TODDLER COLORING BOOK
NUMBERS COLORS SHAPES
numbers shapes counting Coloring

Baby Activity Book for Kids Age 1-3, Boys or Girls
Easy Learning of First Easy Words about Shapes and Numbers

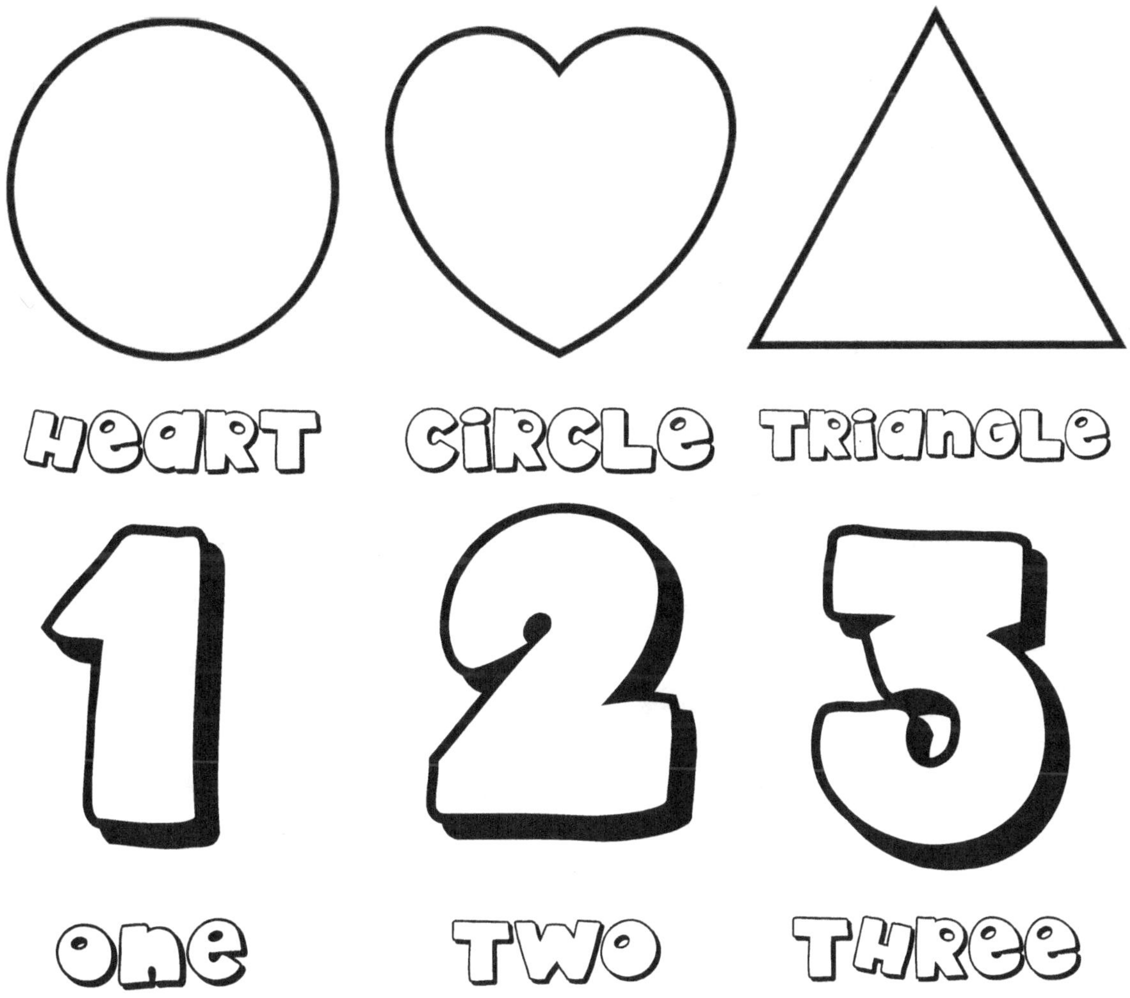

Copyright 2018

All rights reserved. No part of this publication may be reproduced, stored in a retrieval system, or transmitted in any form or by any means, electronic, mechanical, photocopying, recording or otherwise, without the prior written permission of the publisher.

Printed by CreateSpace, An Amazon.com Company
A Publication by Coloring Books For Toddlers

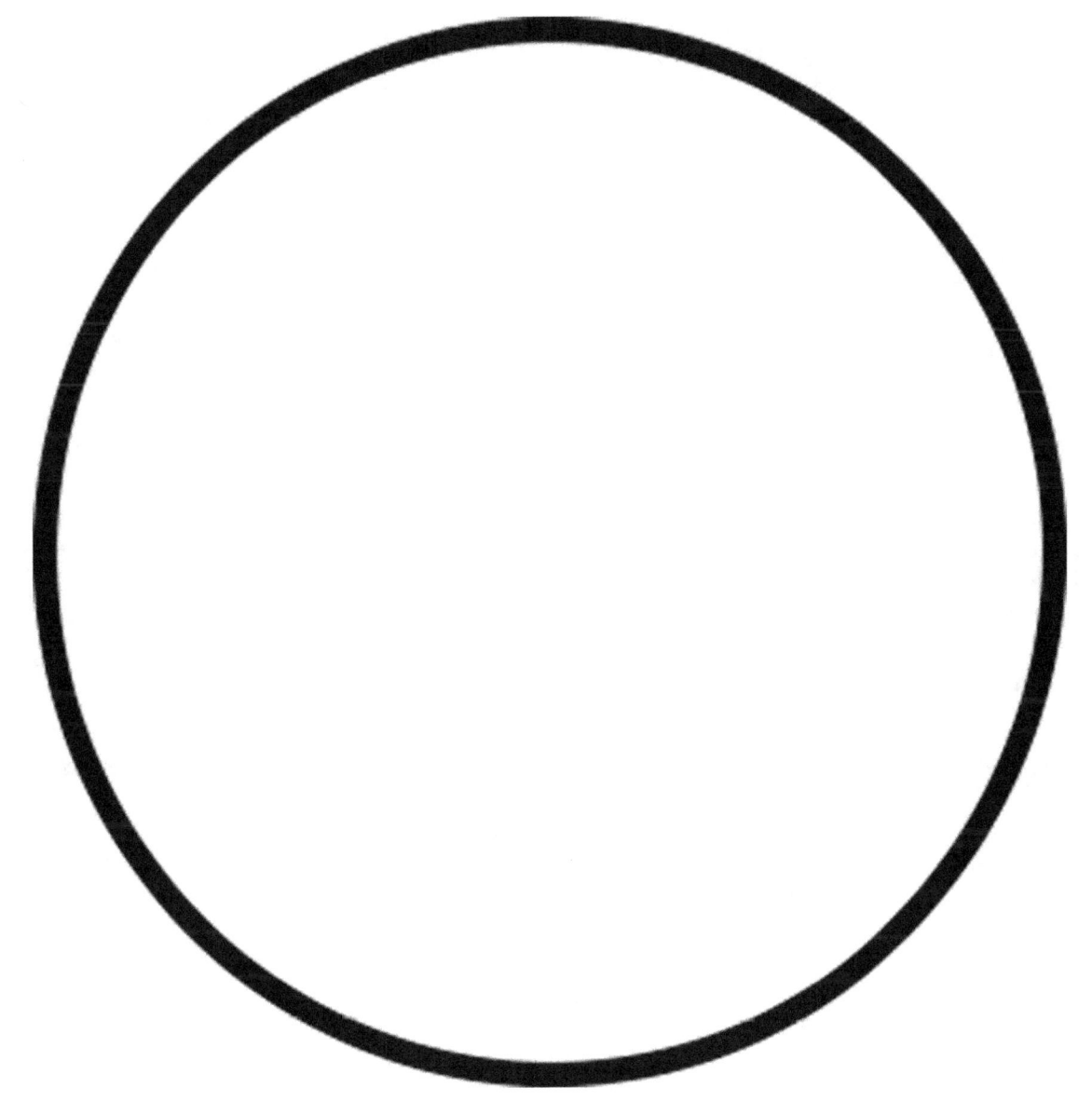

SQUARE

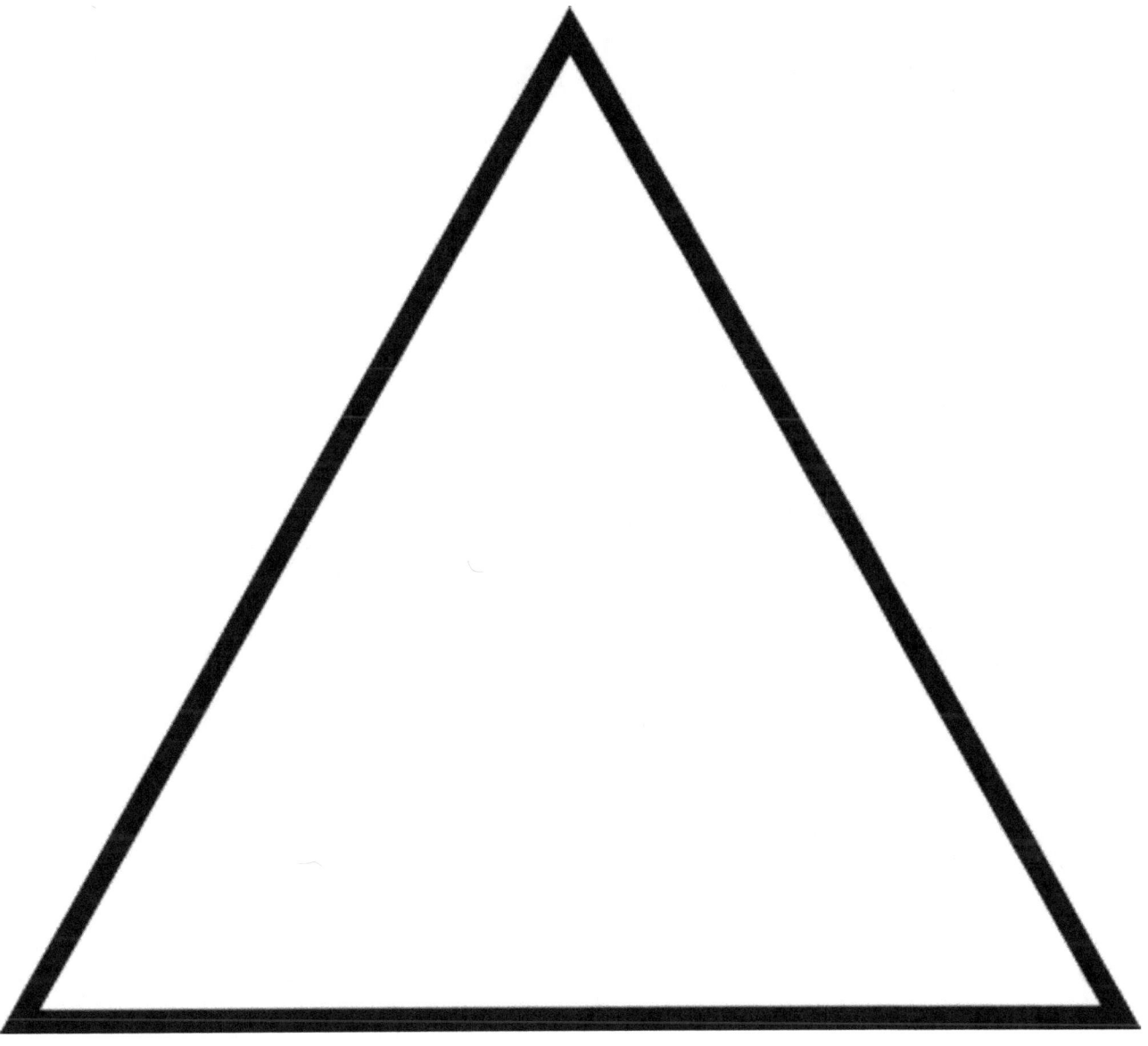

TRIANGLE

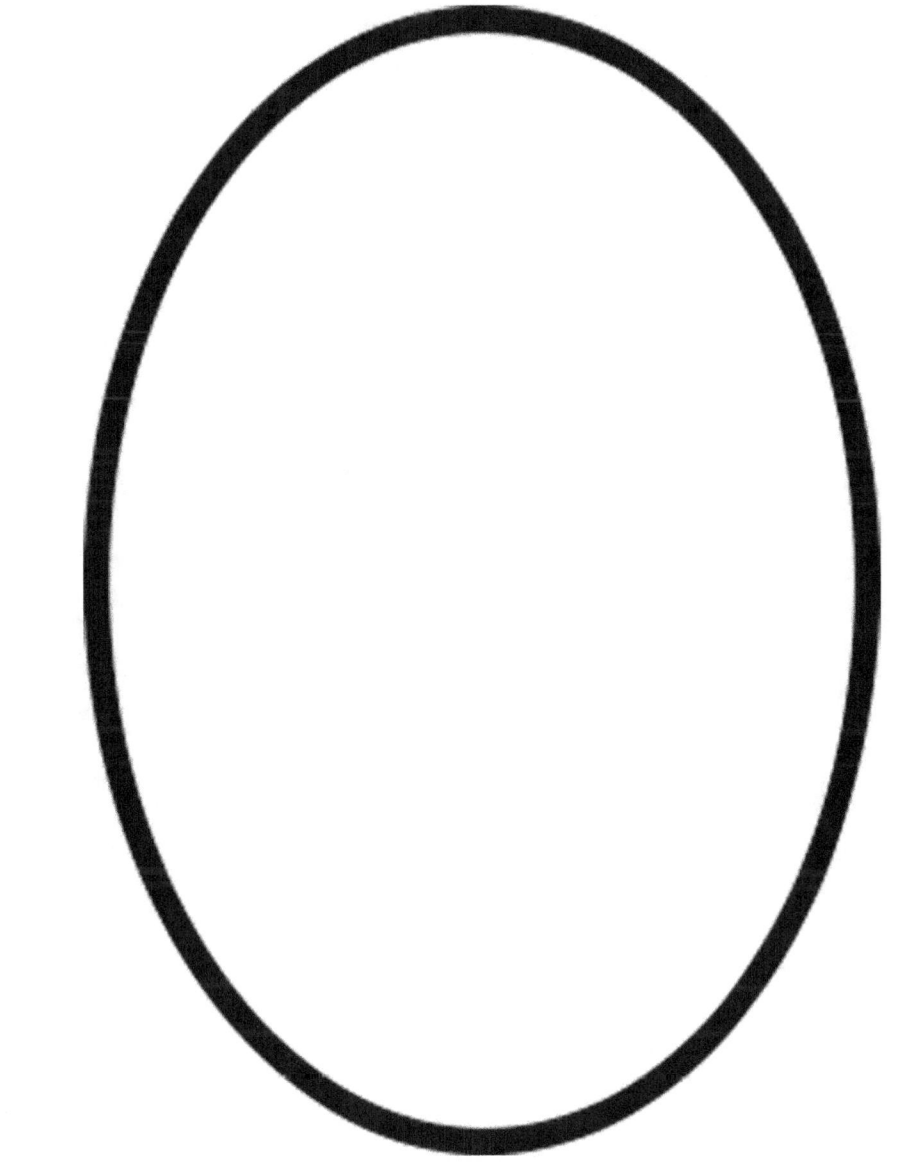

ellipse

RECTANGLE

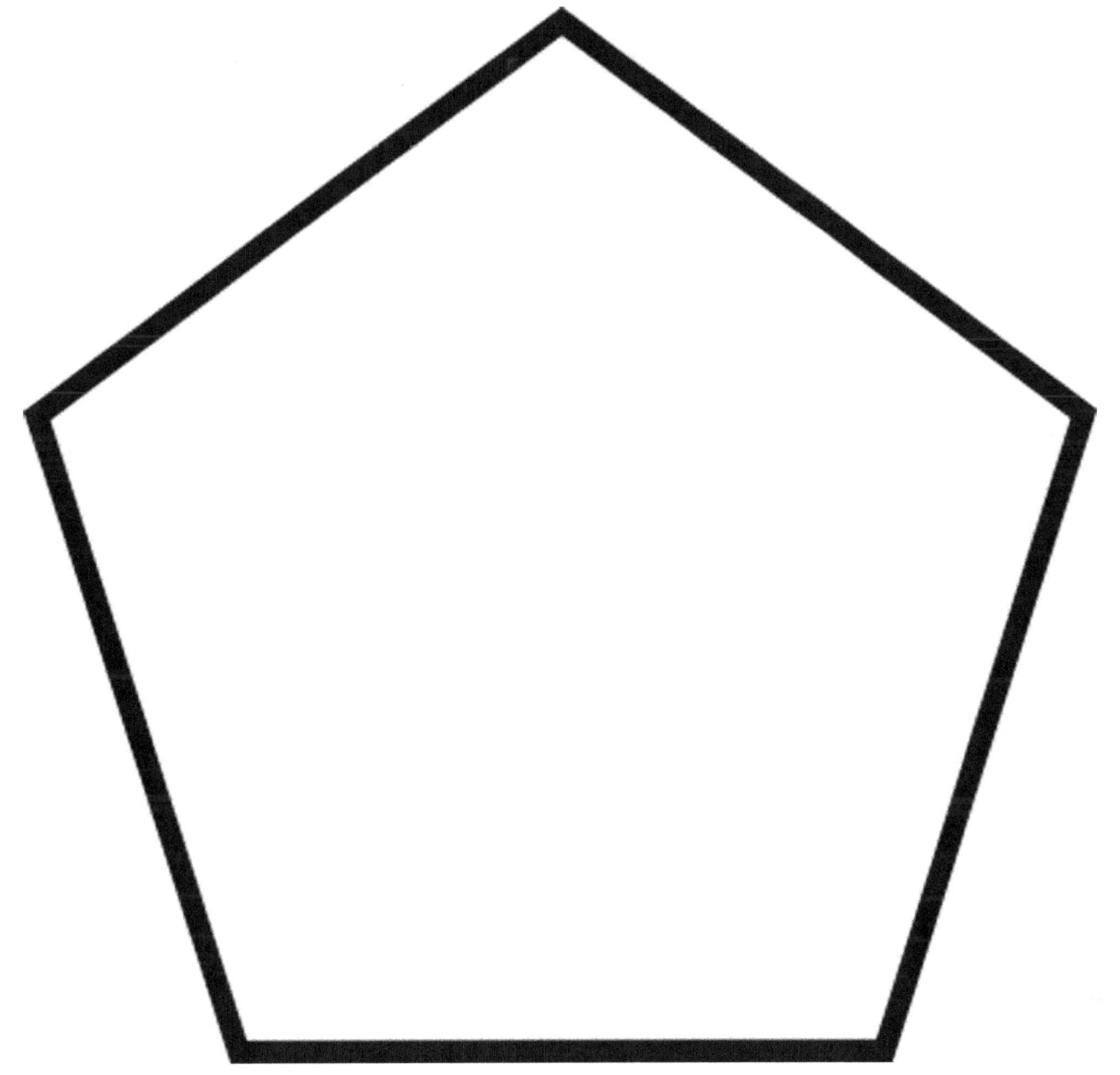

pentagon

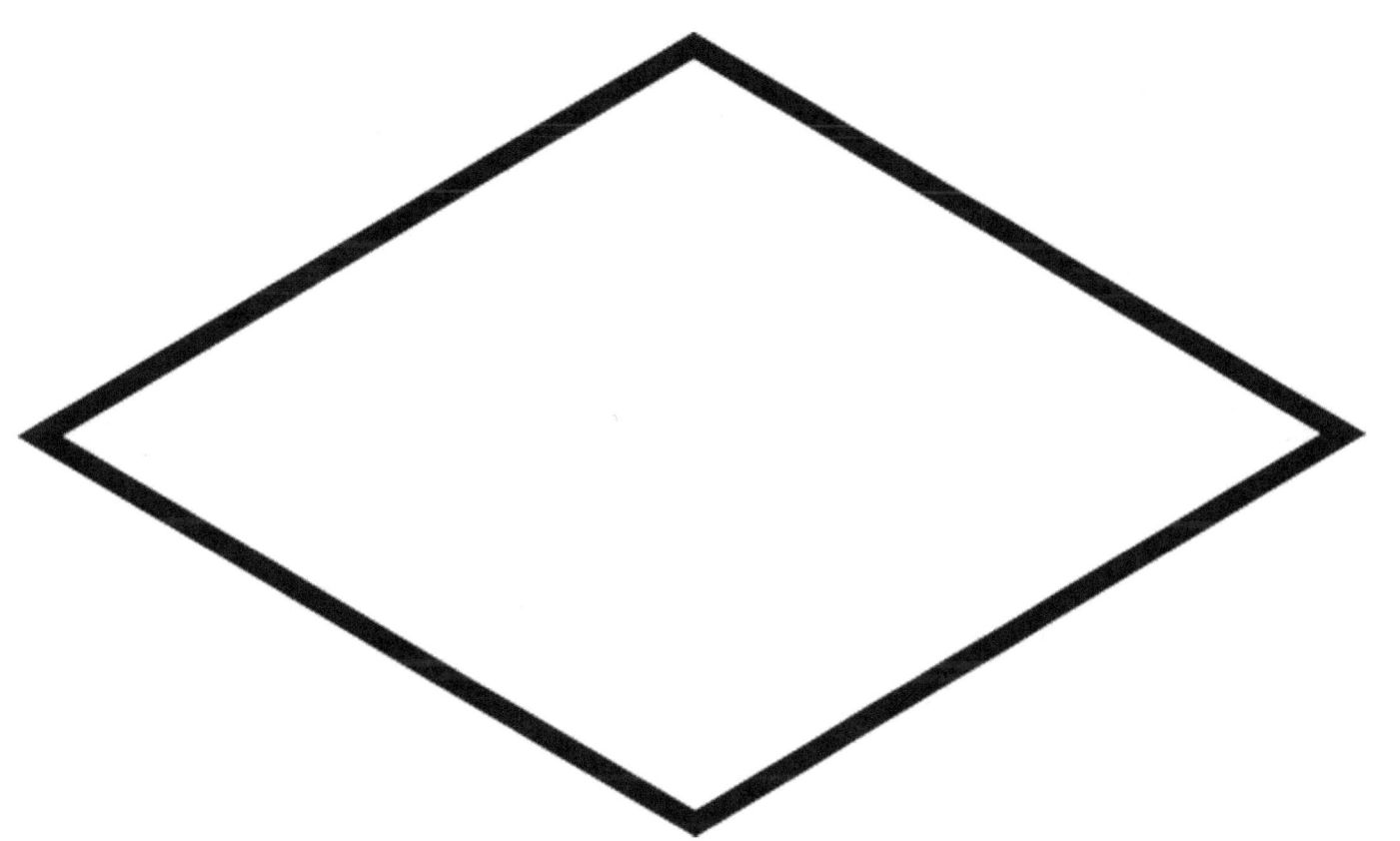

Diamond

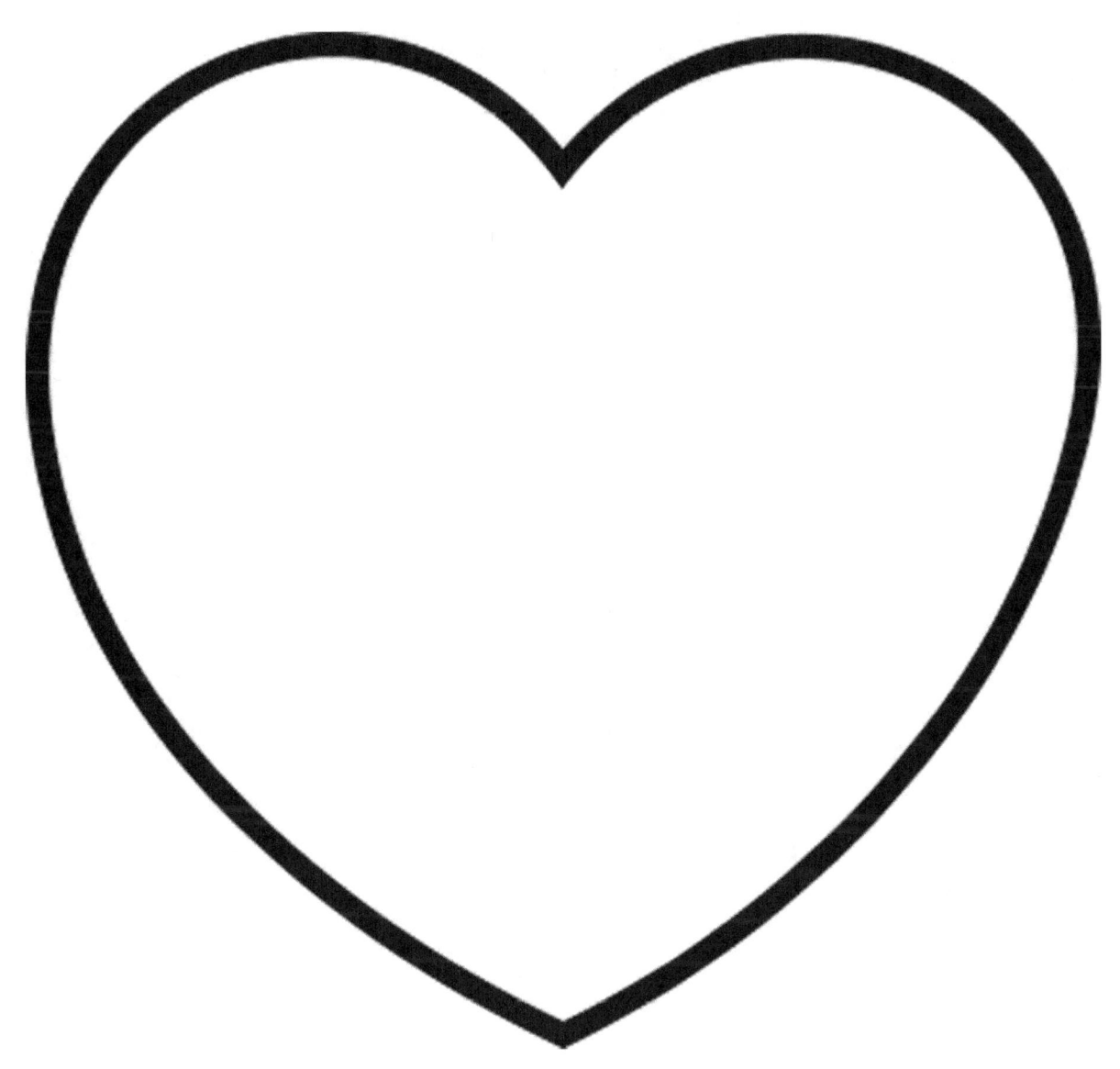

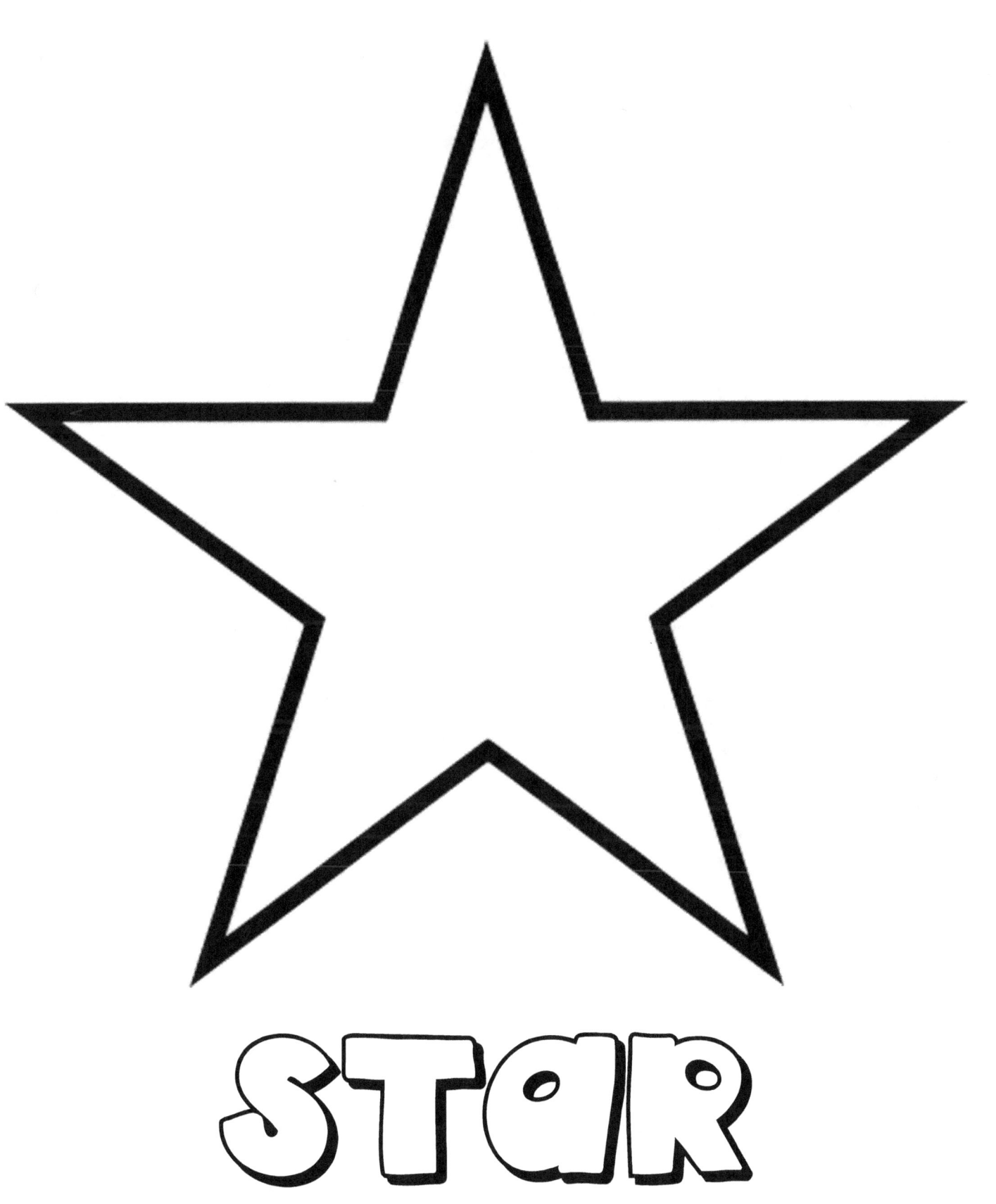

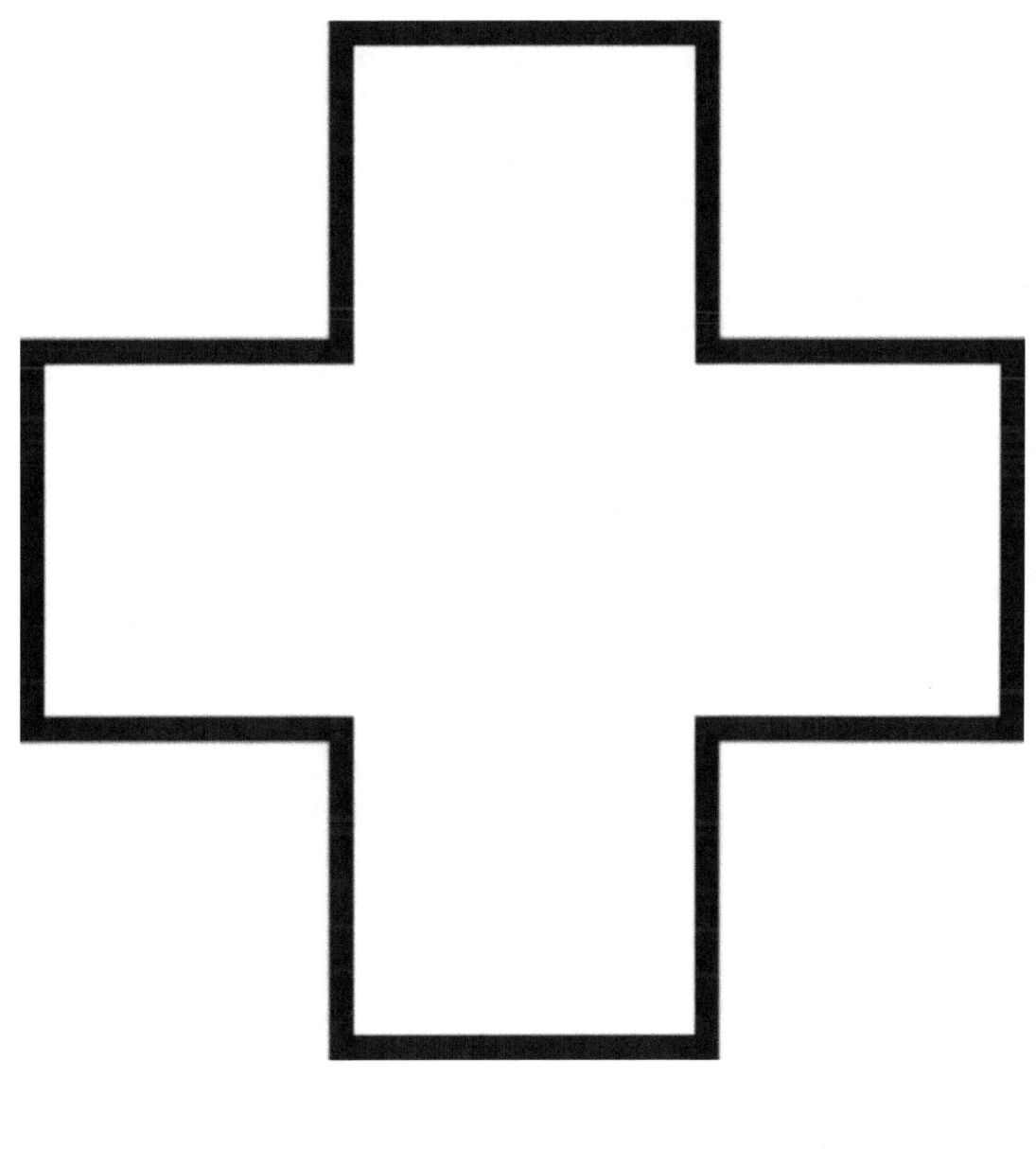

CROSS

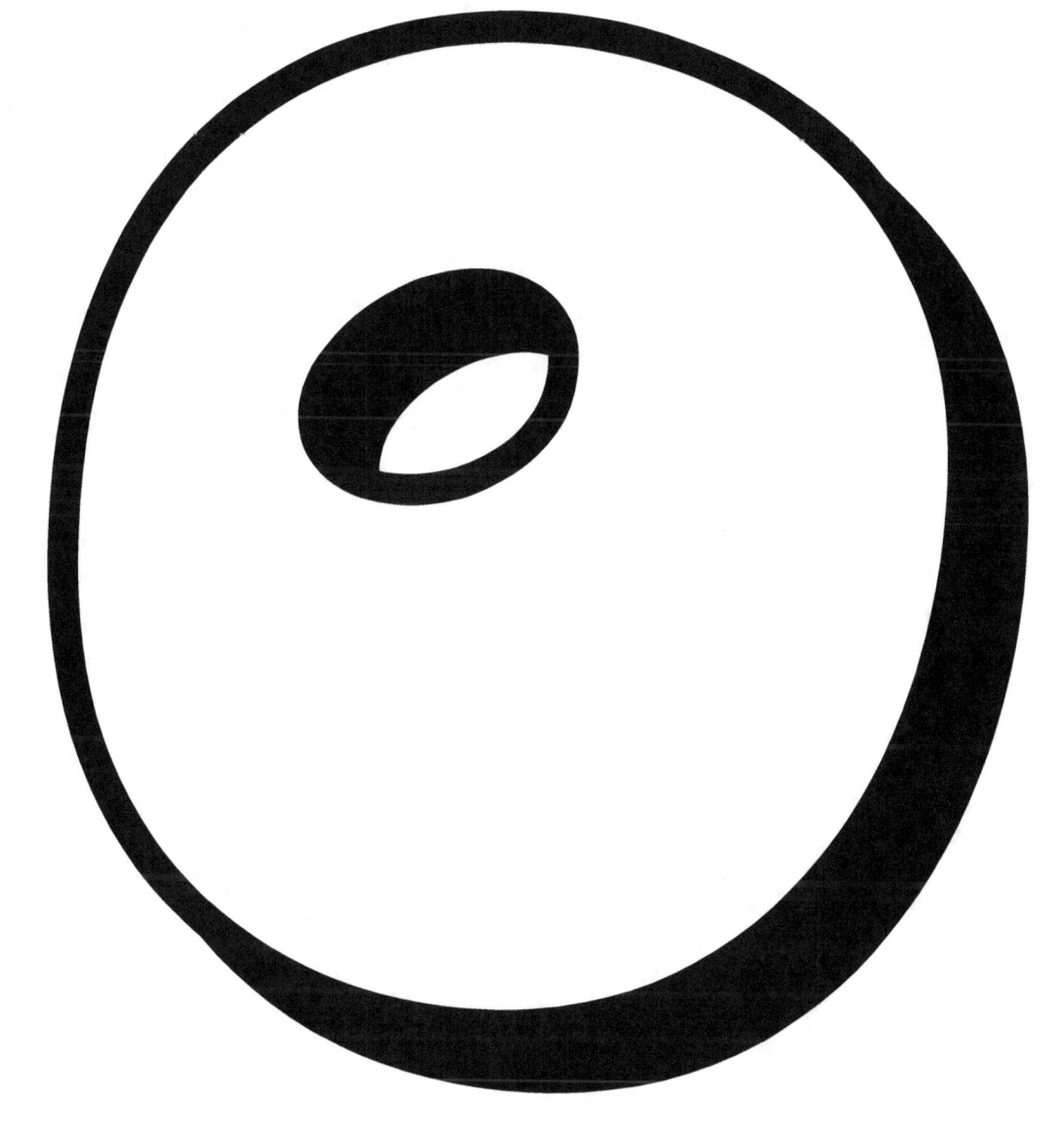

1

one

2
TWO

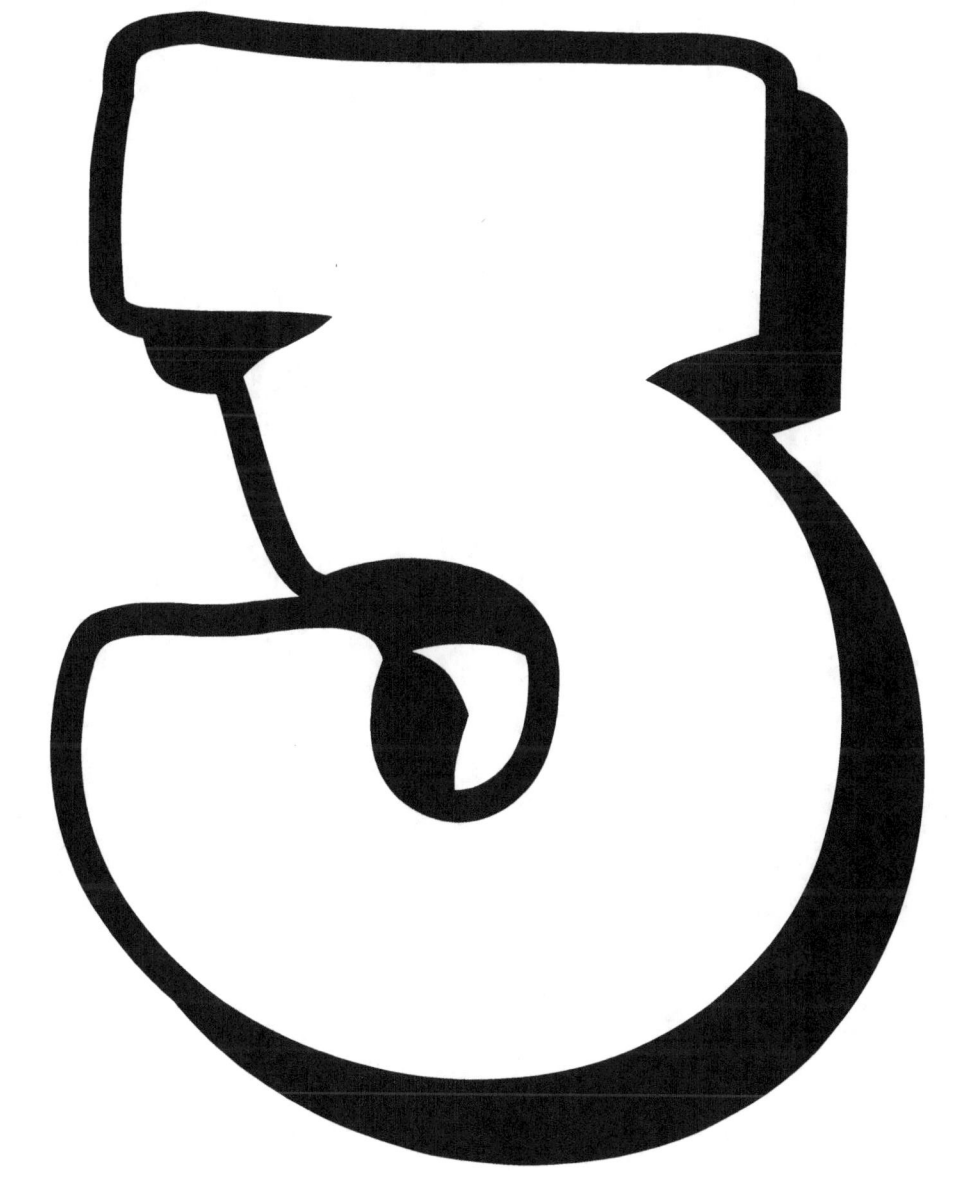

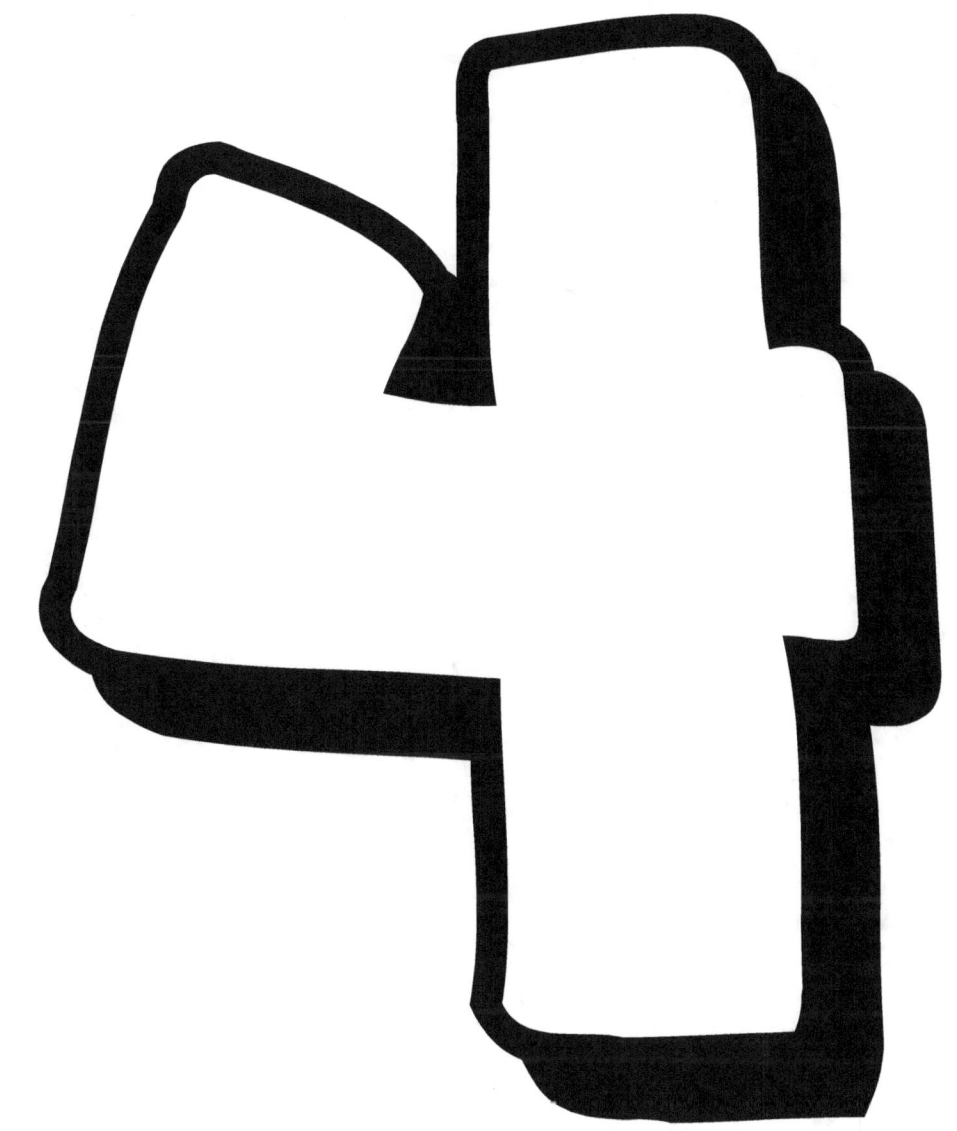

FOUR

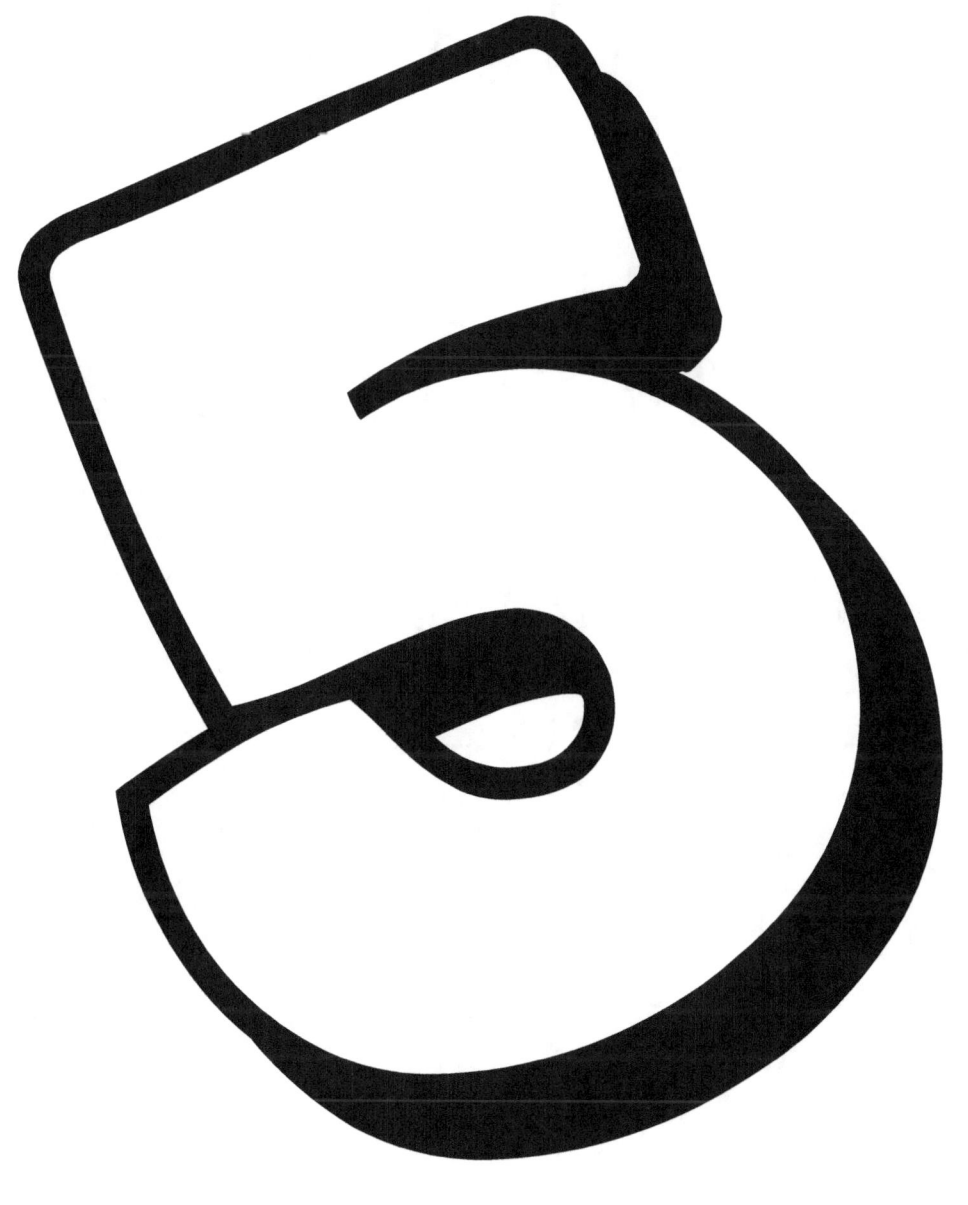

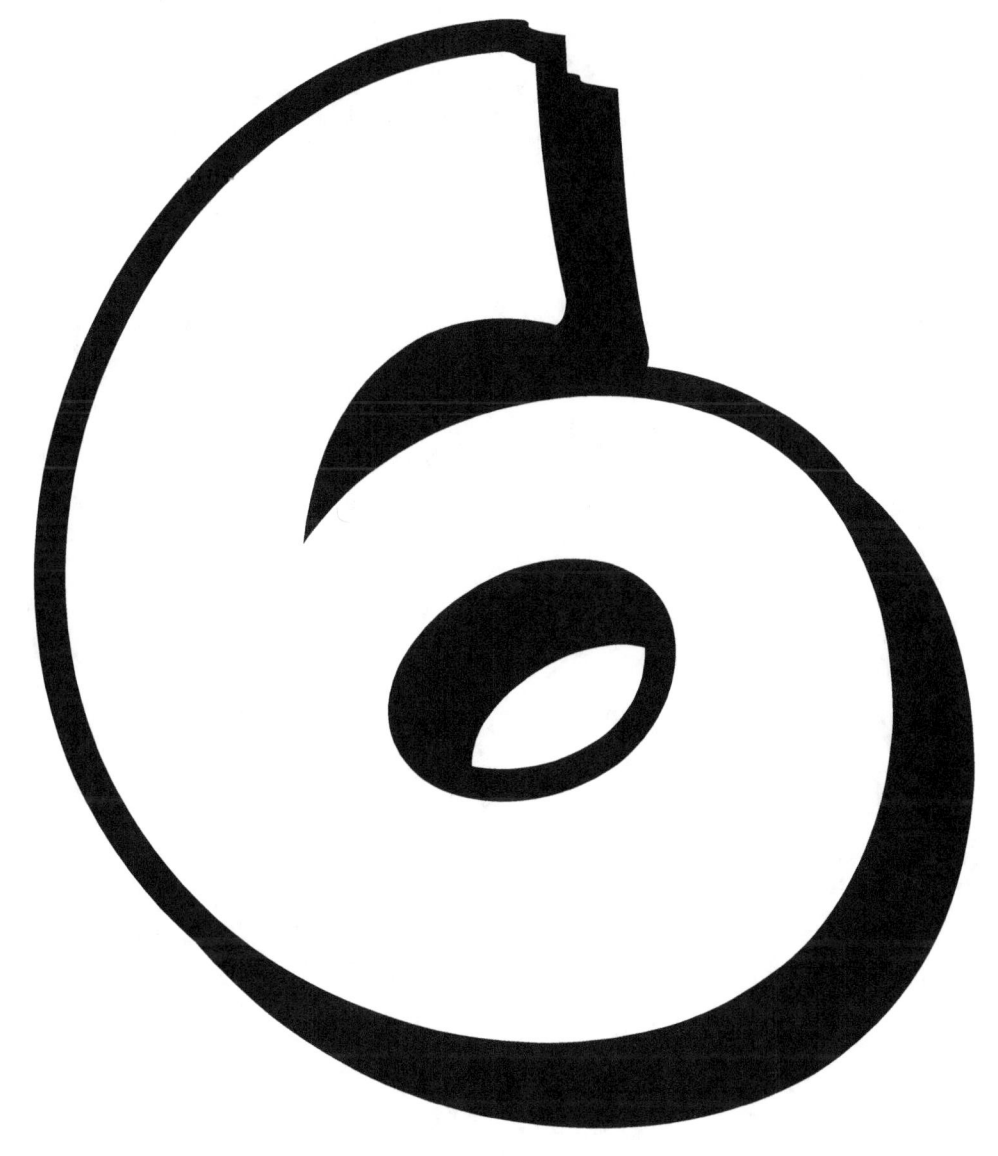

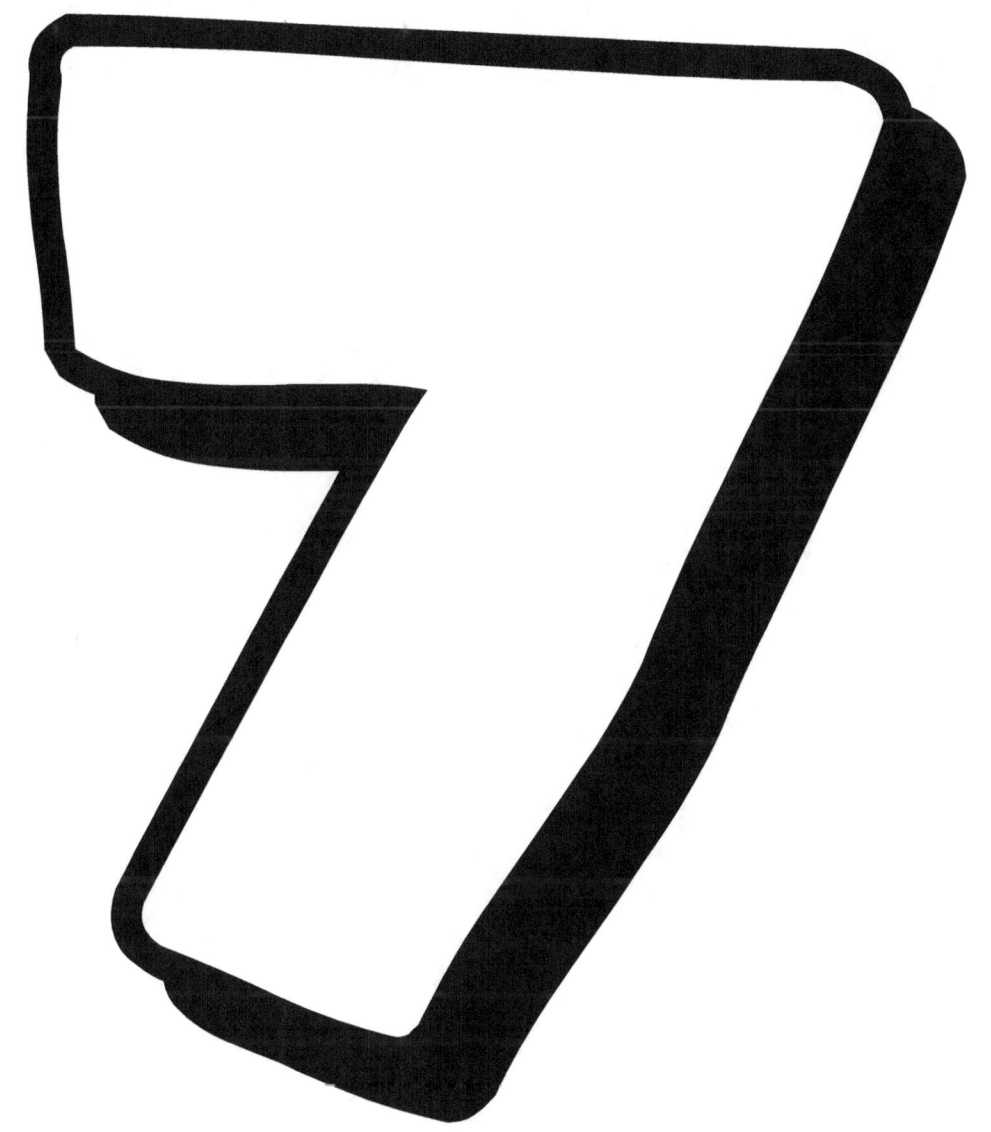

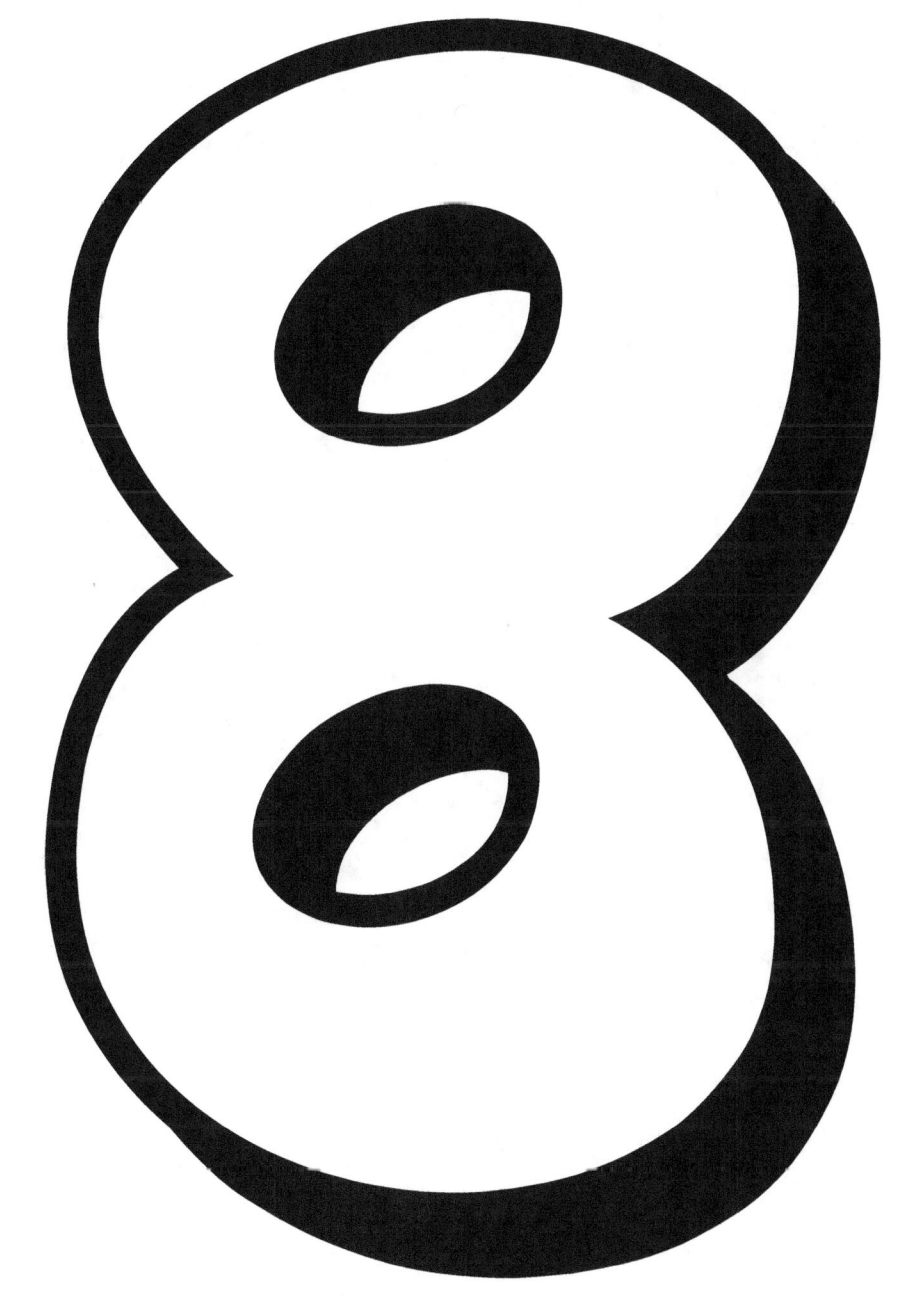

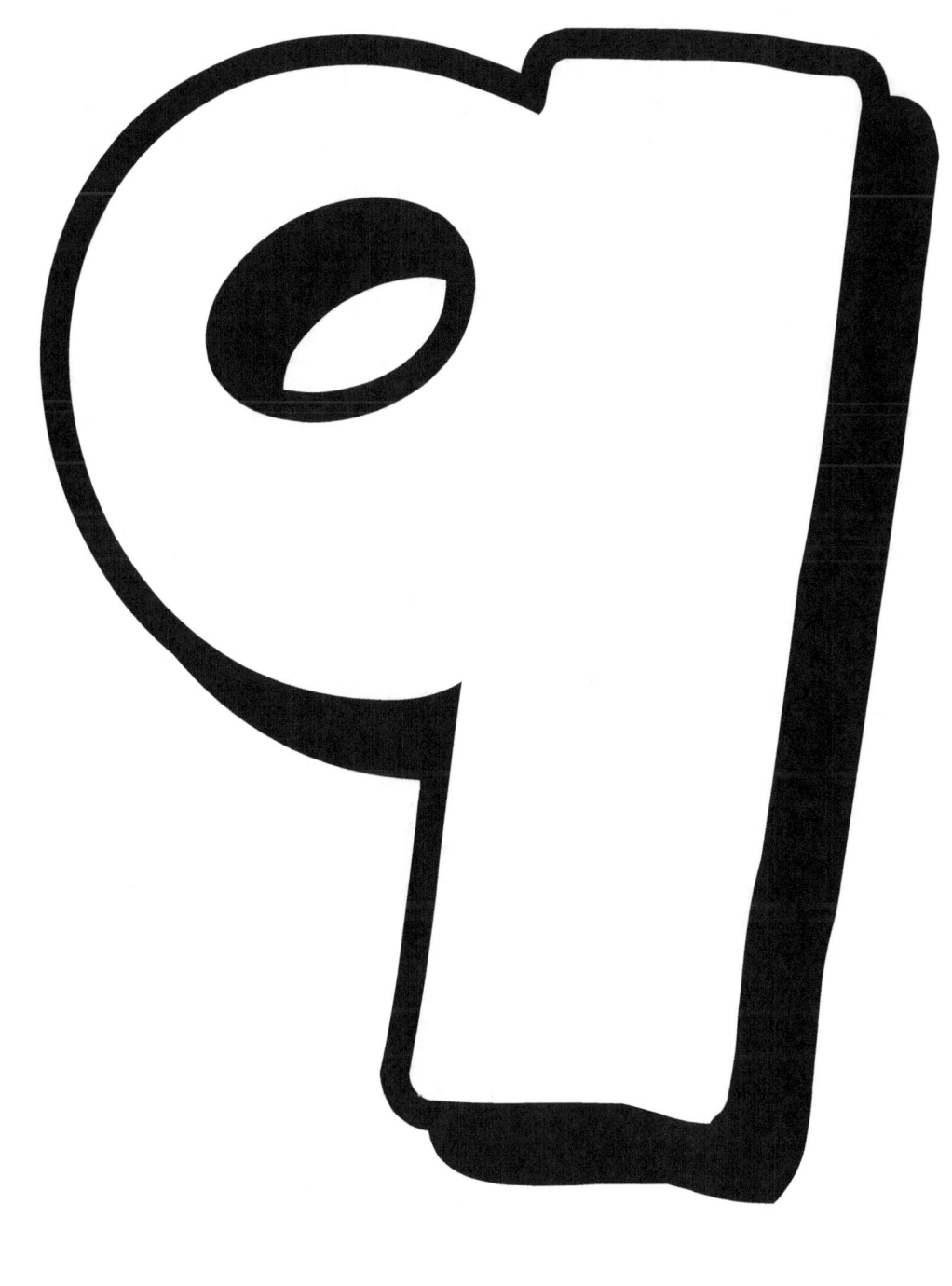

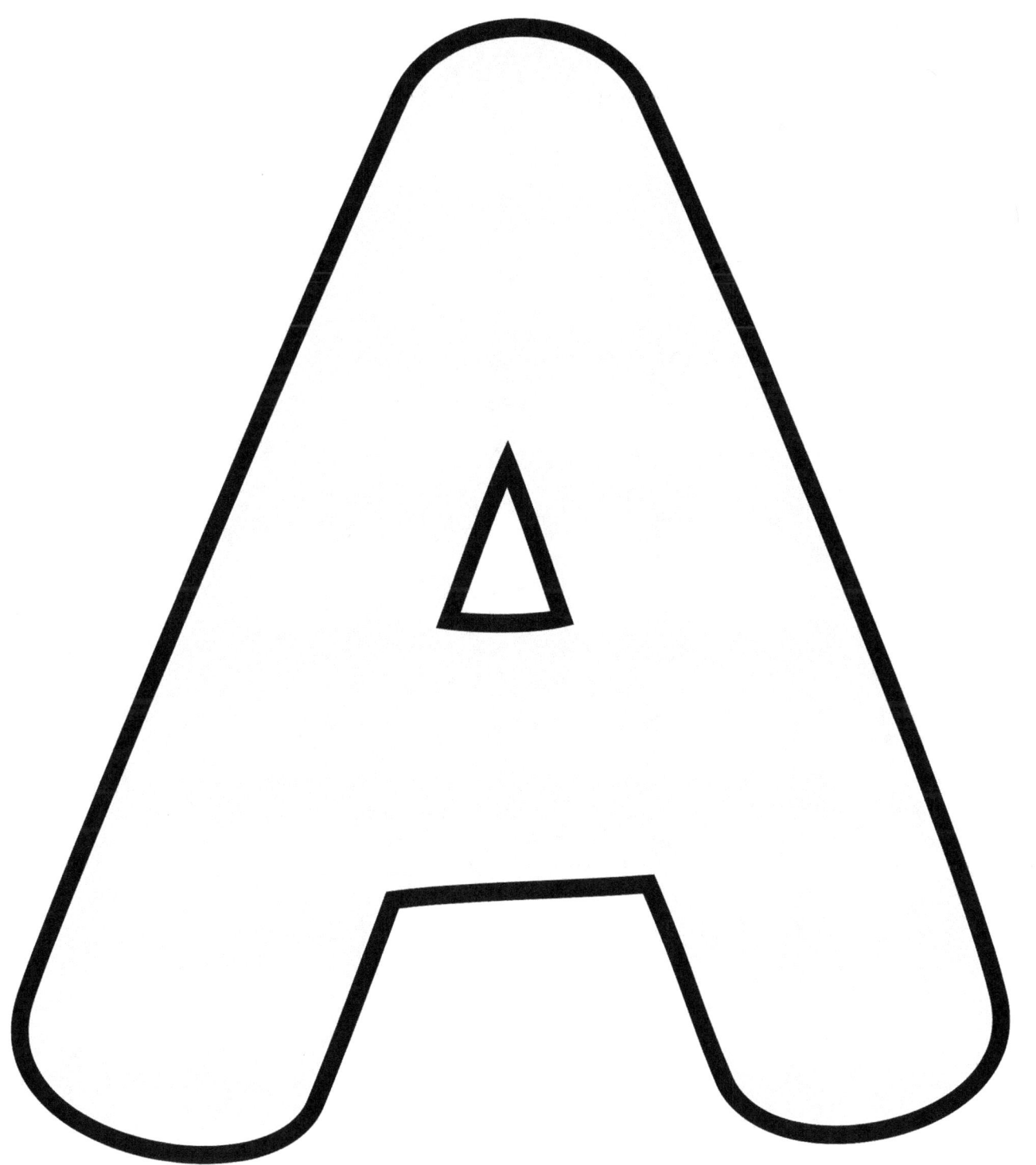

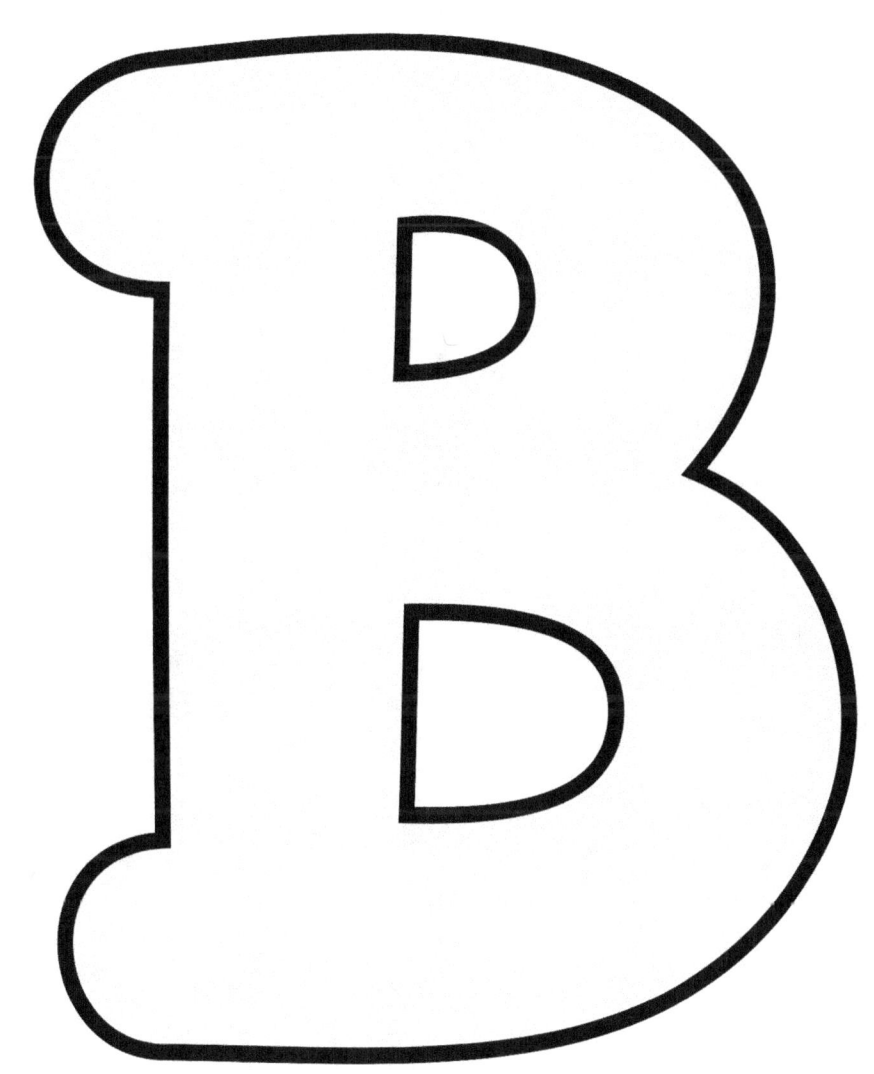

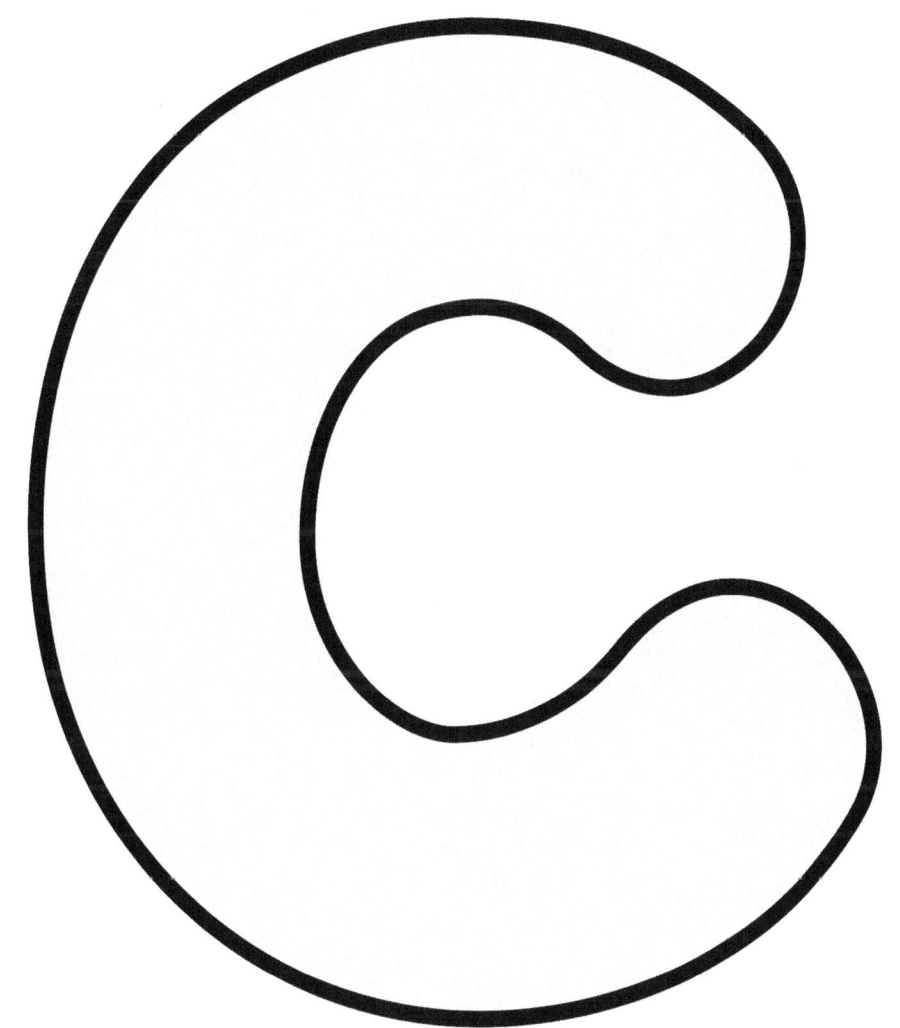

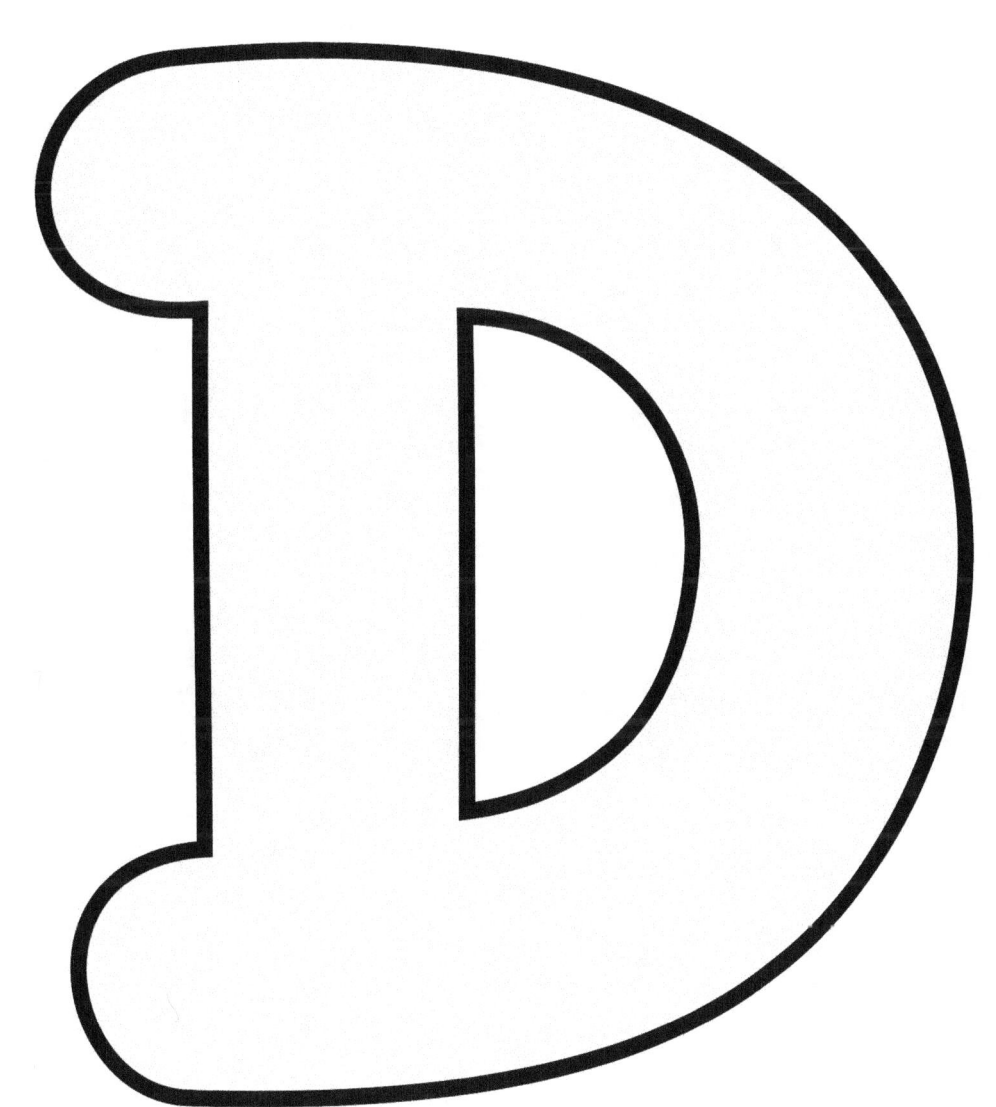

E

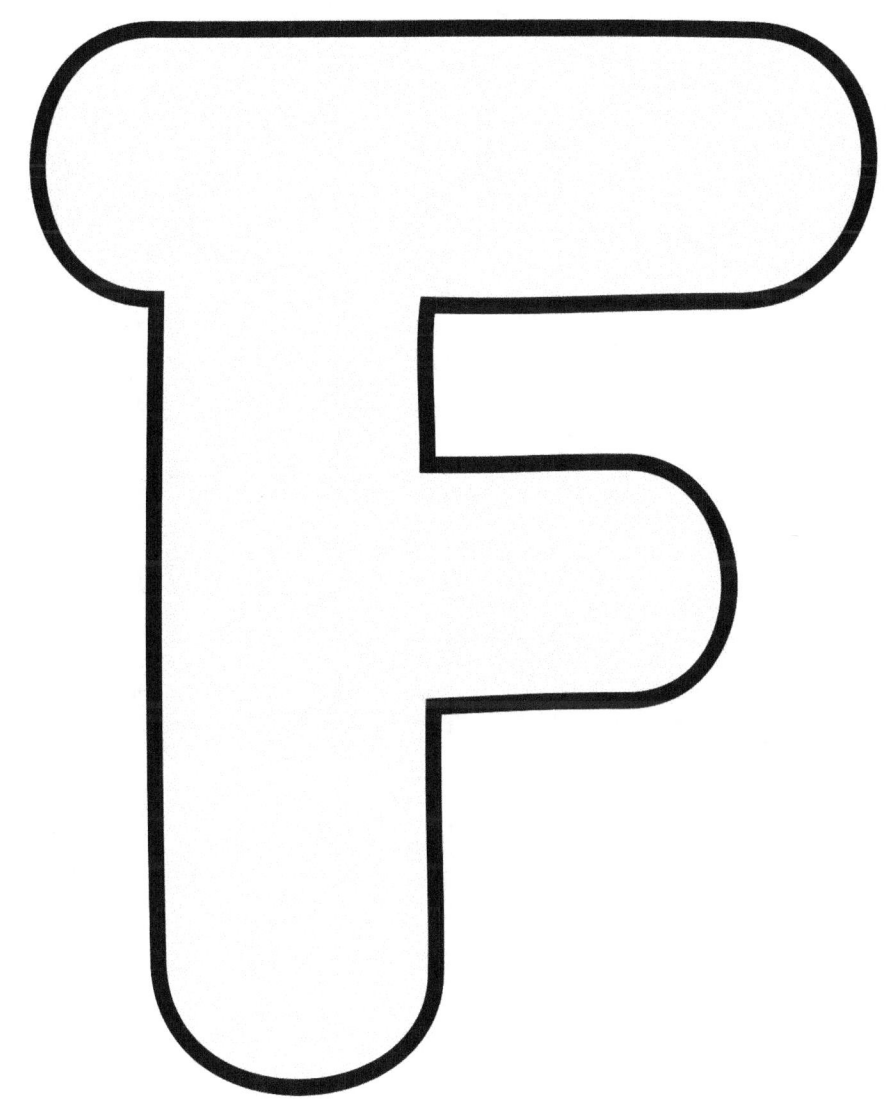

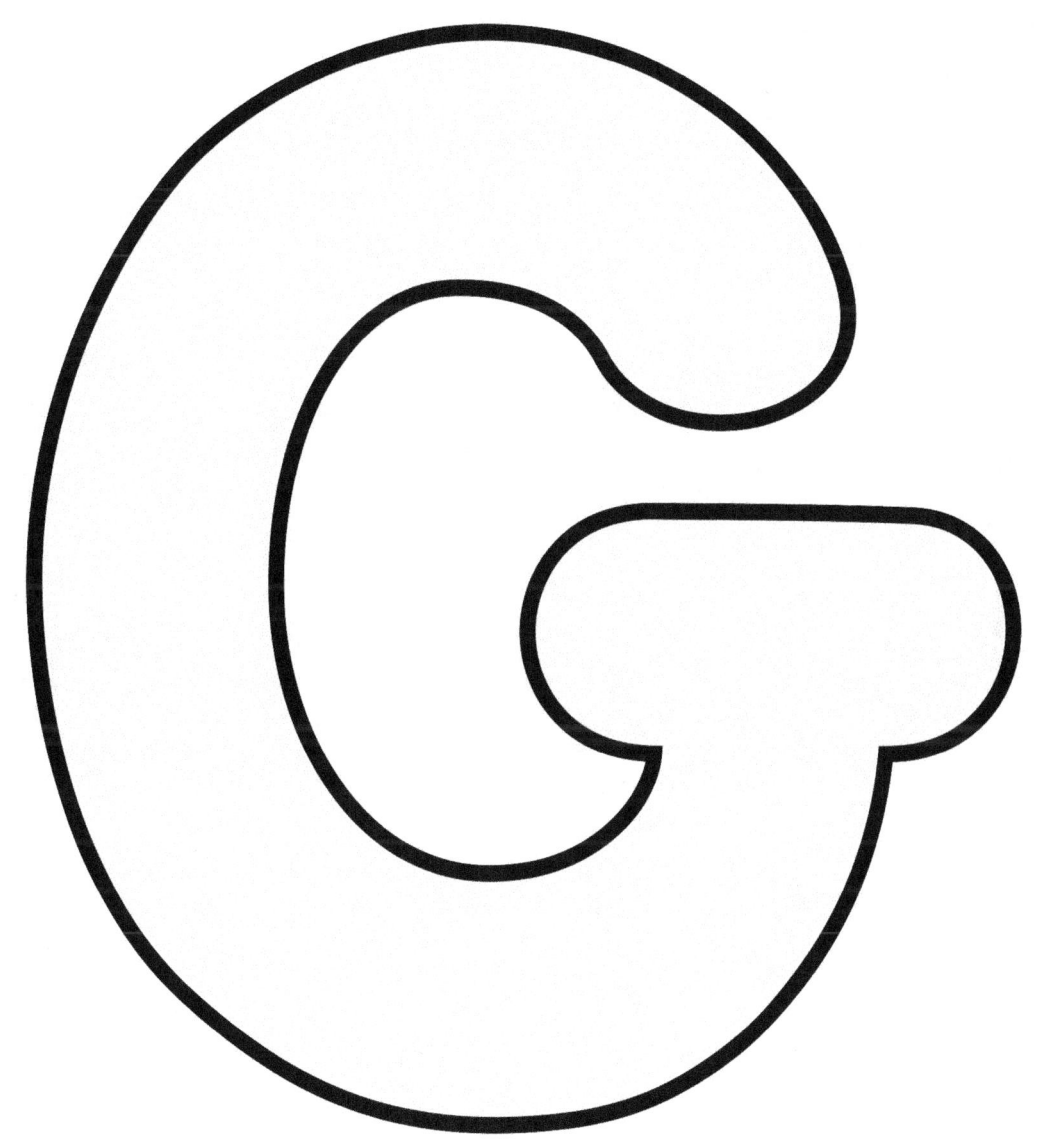

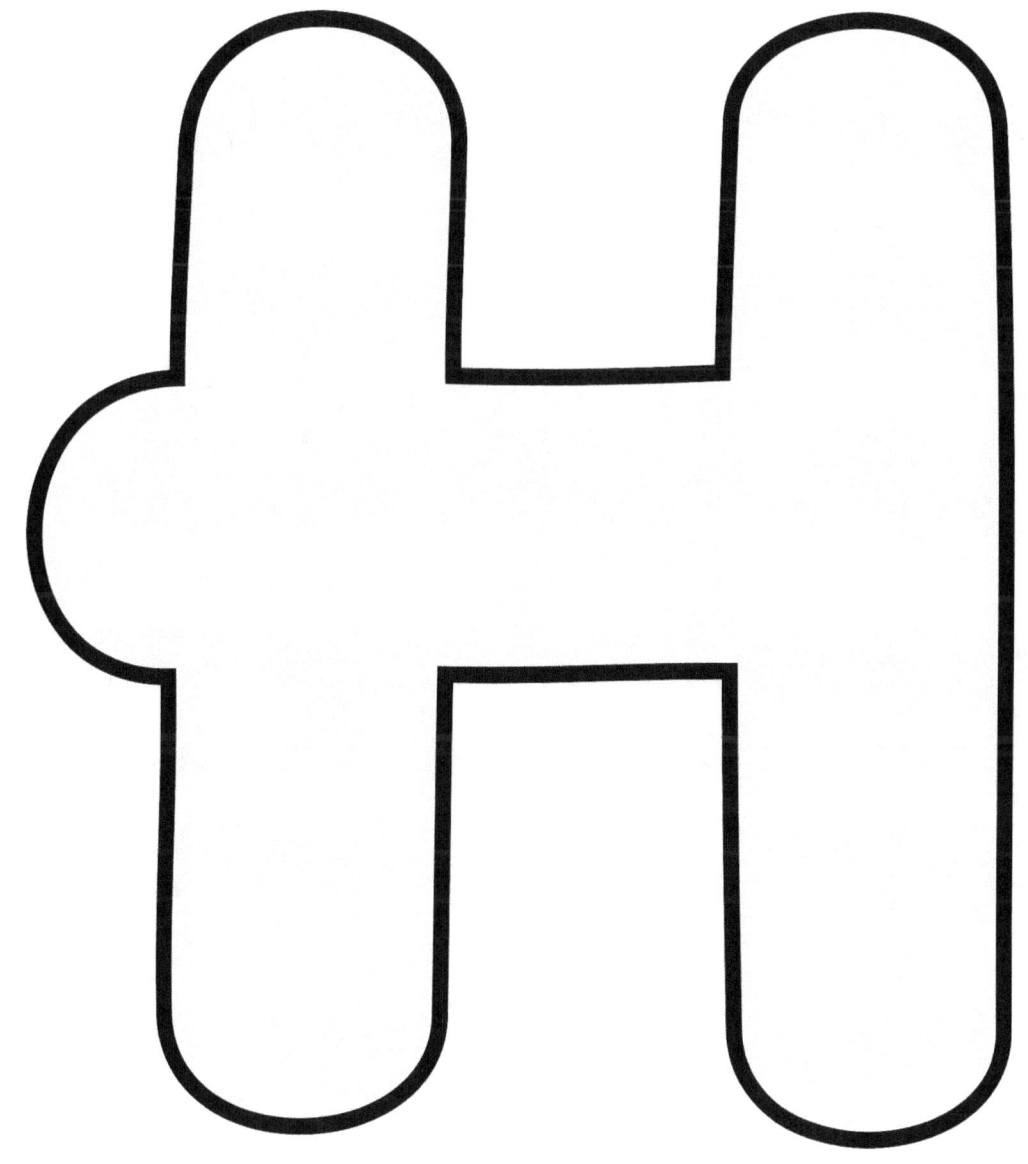

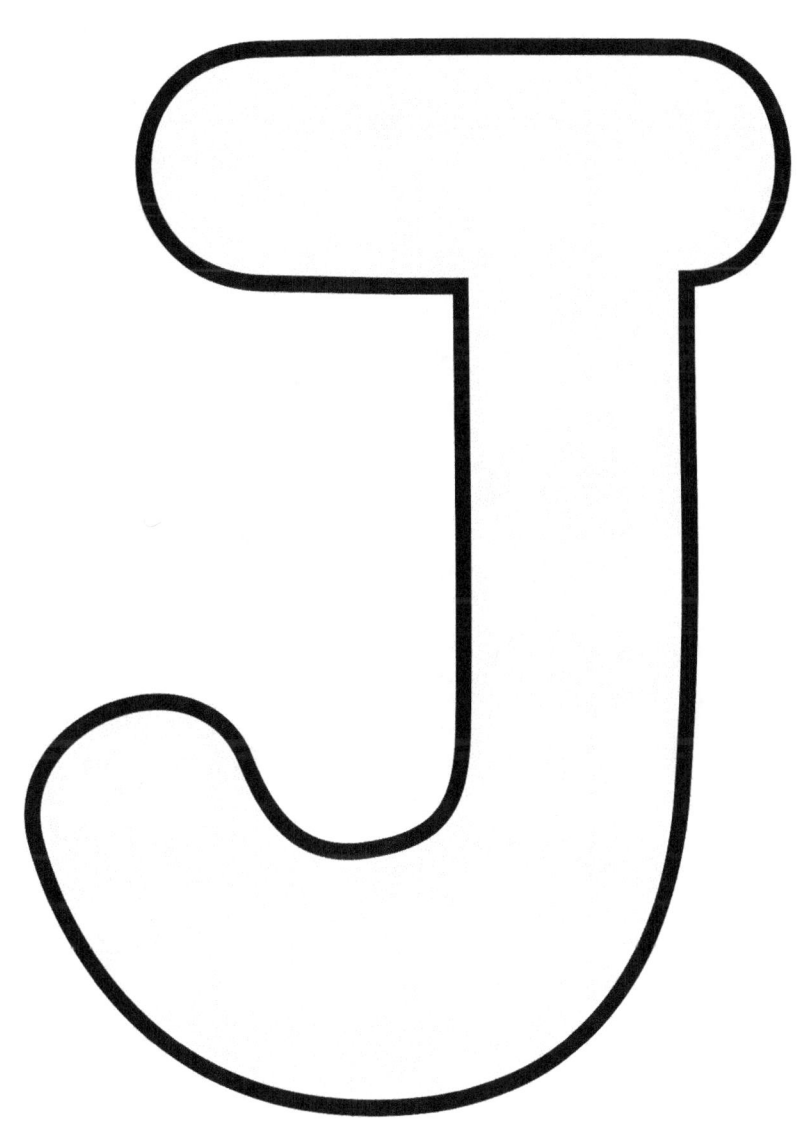

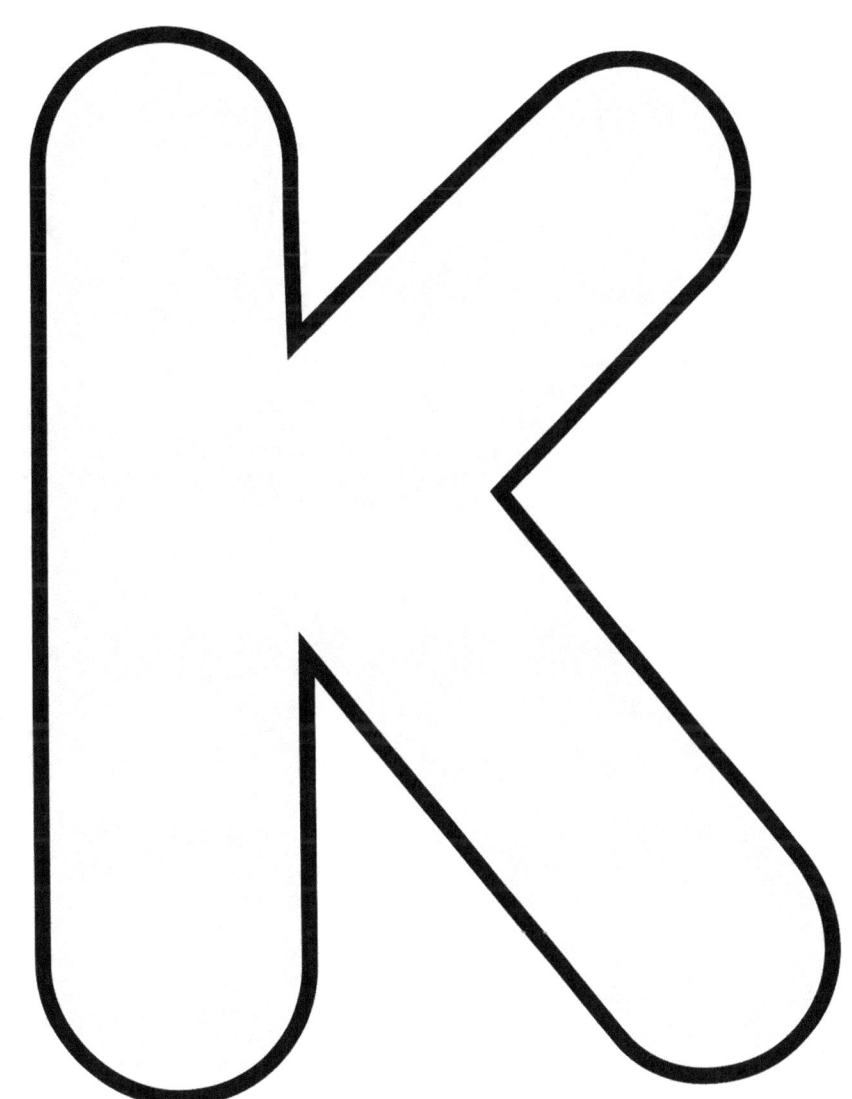

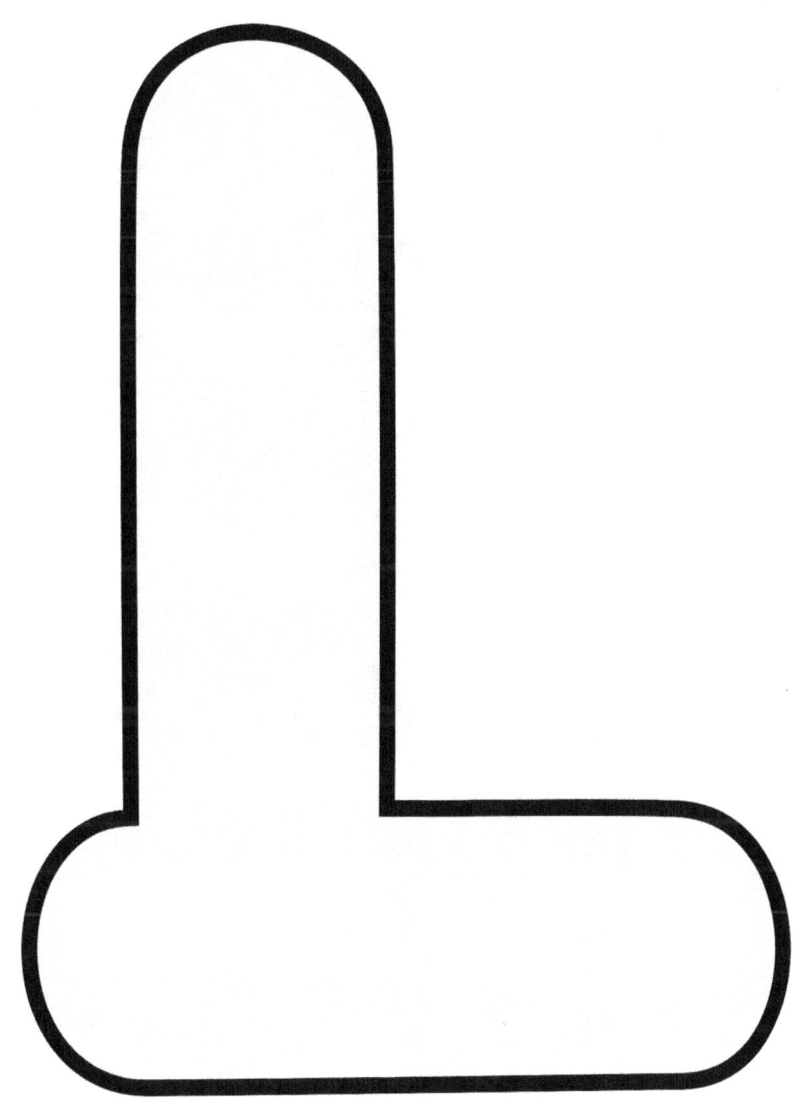

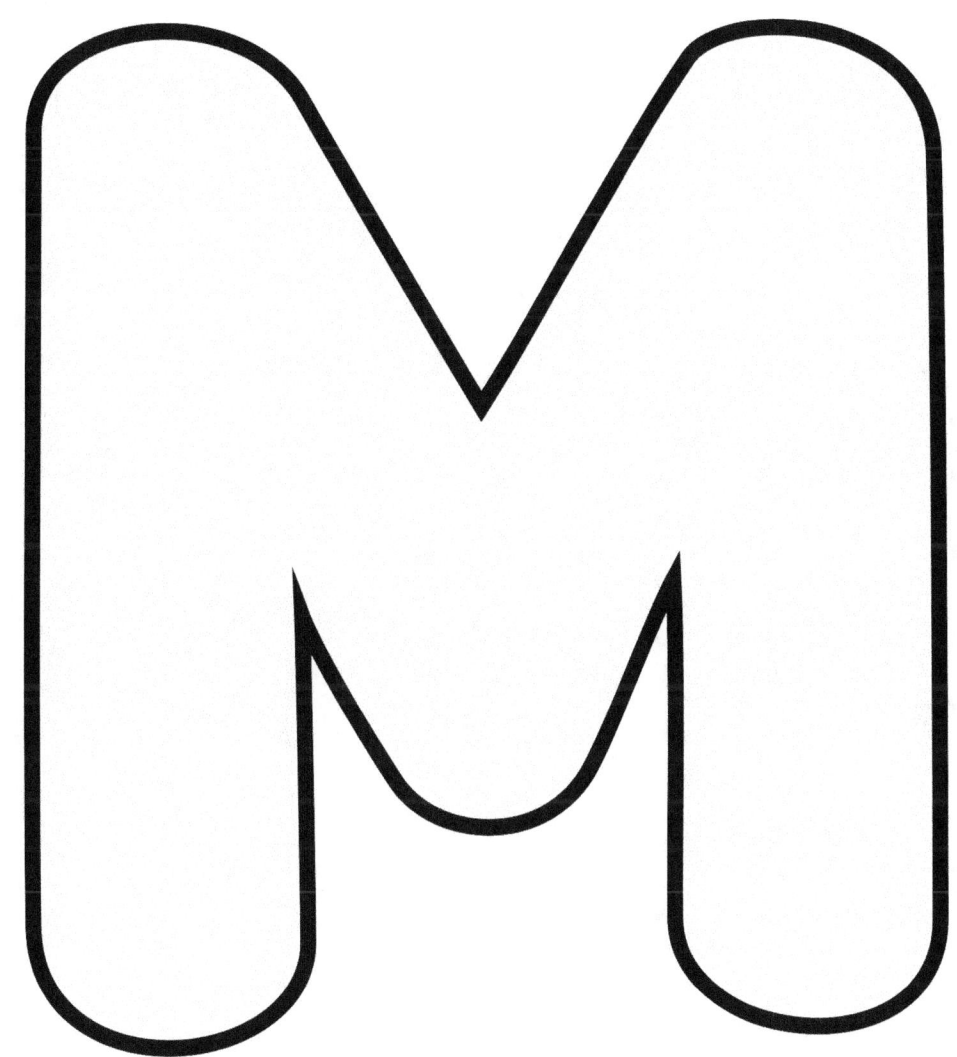

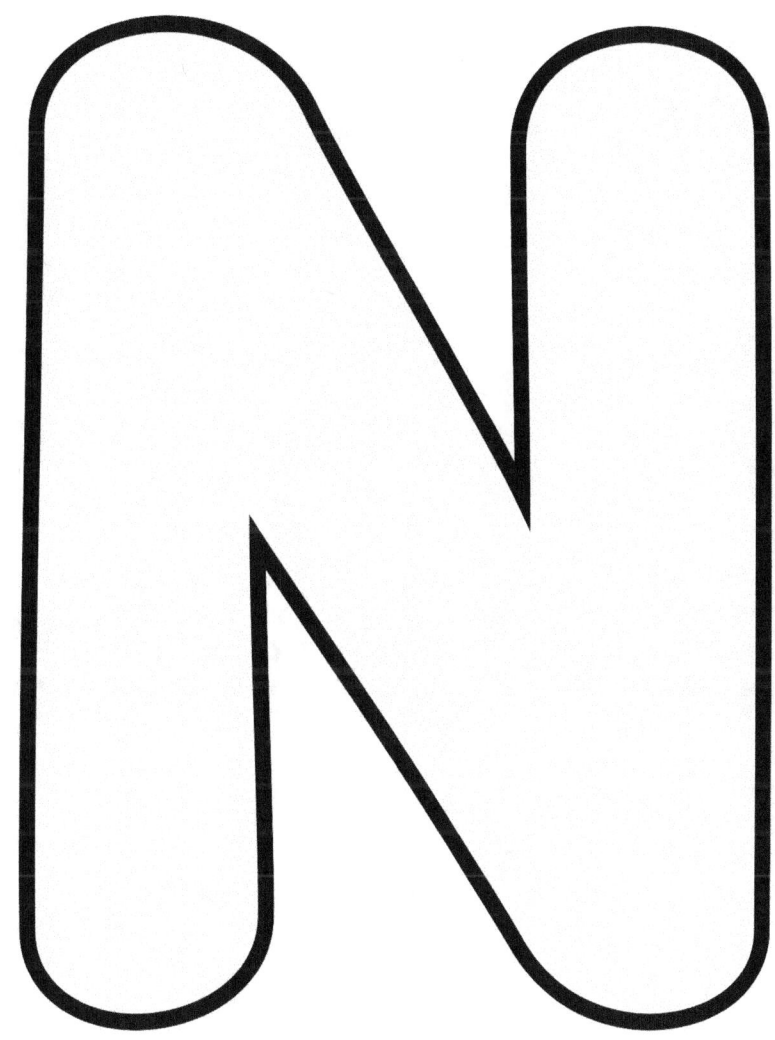

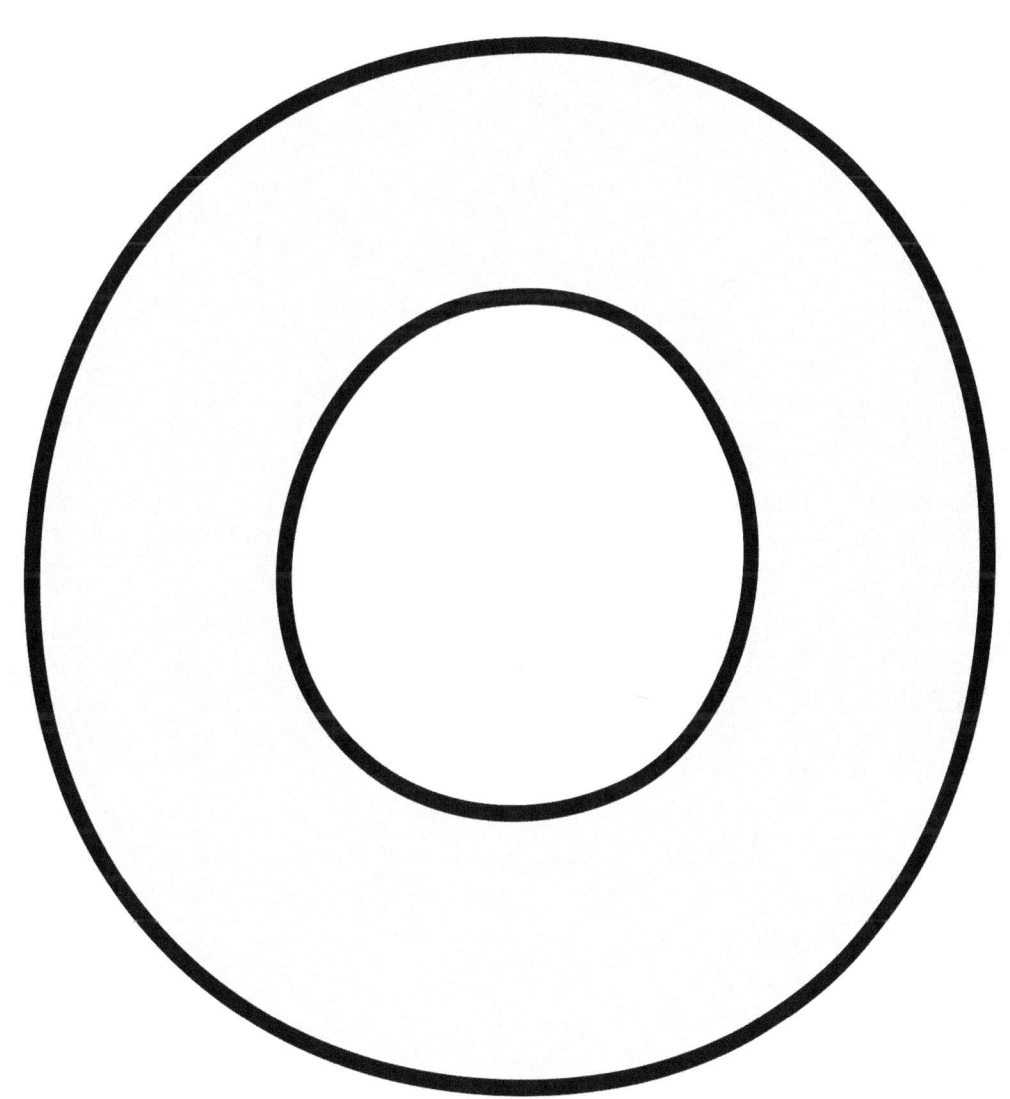

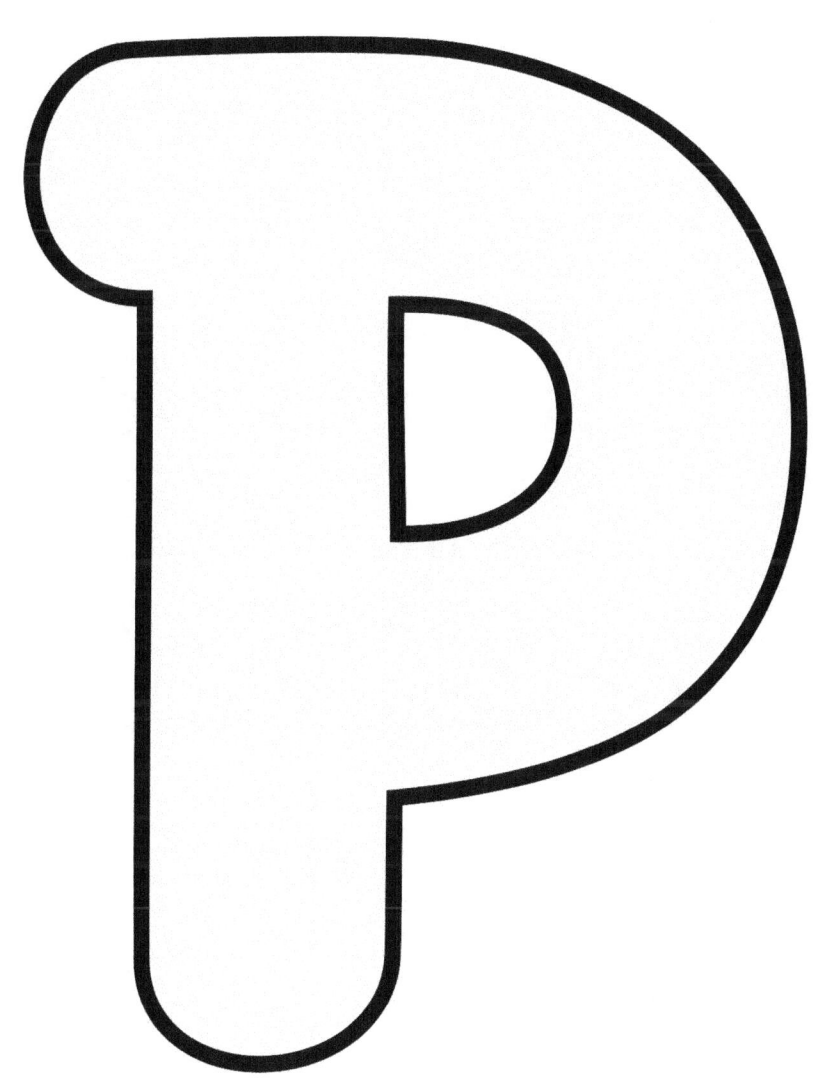

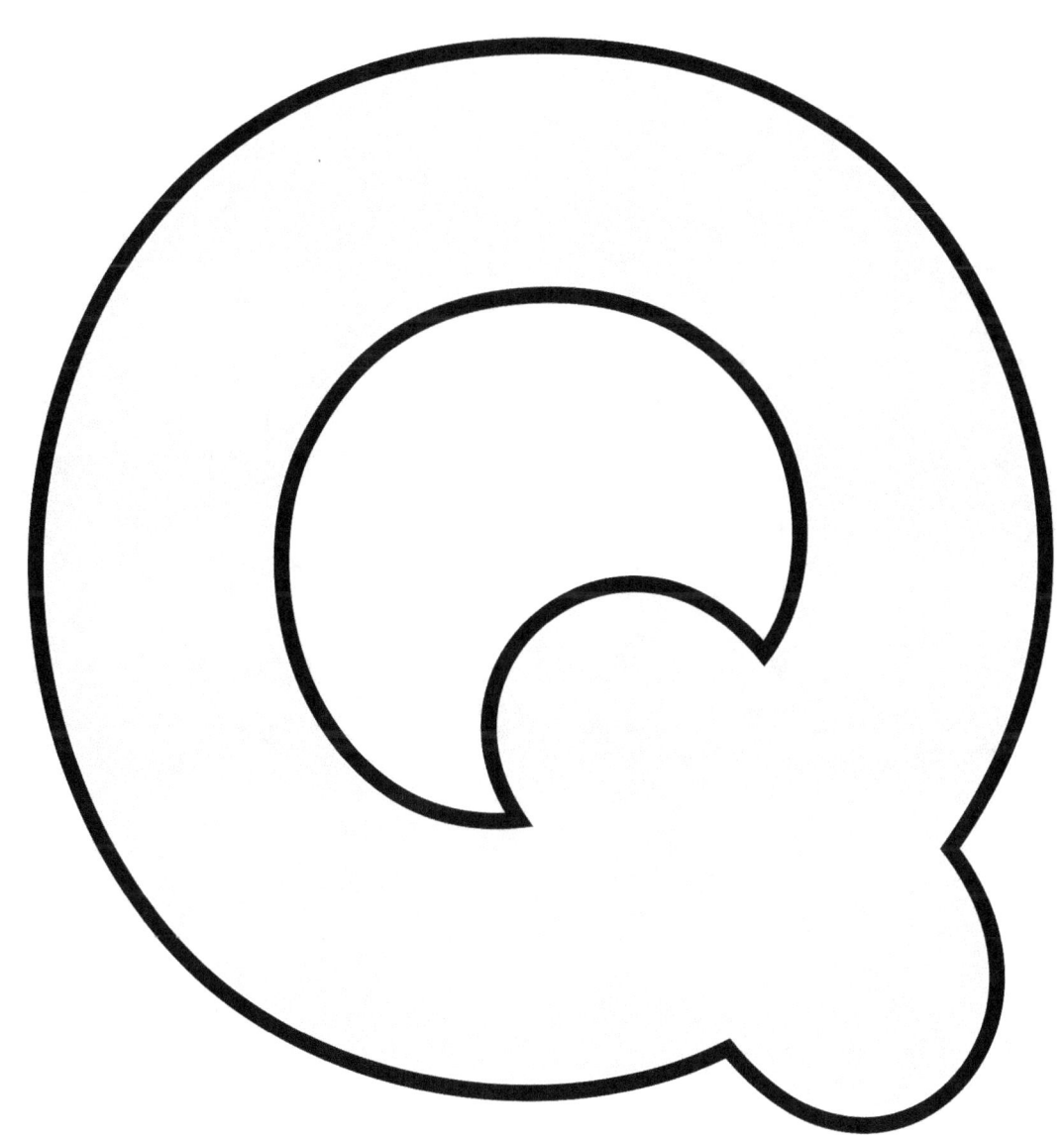

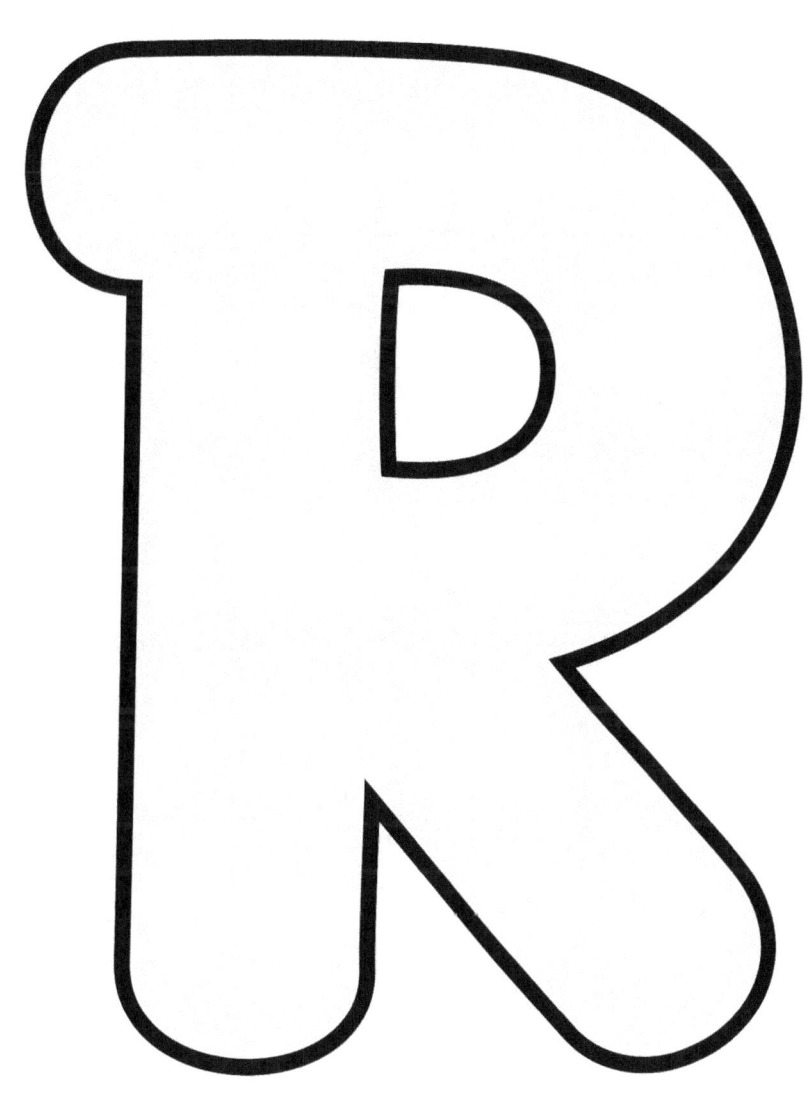

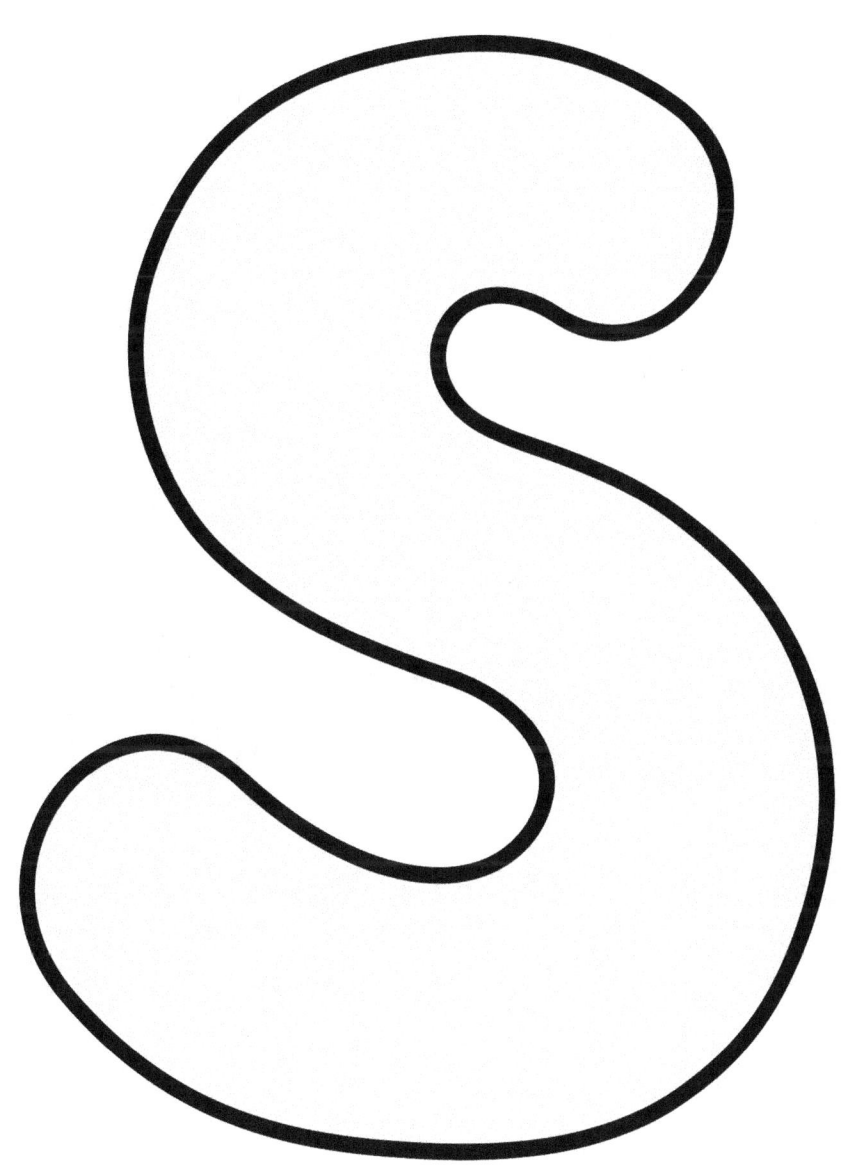

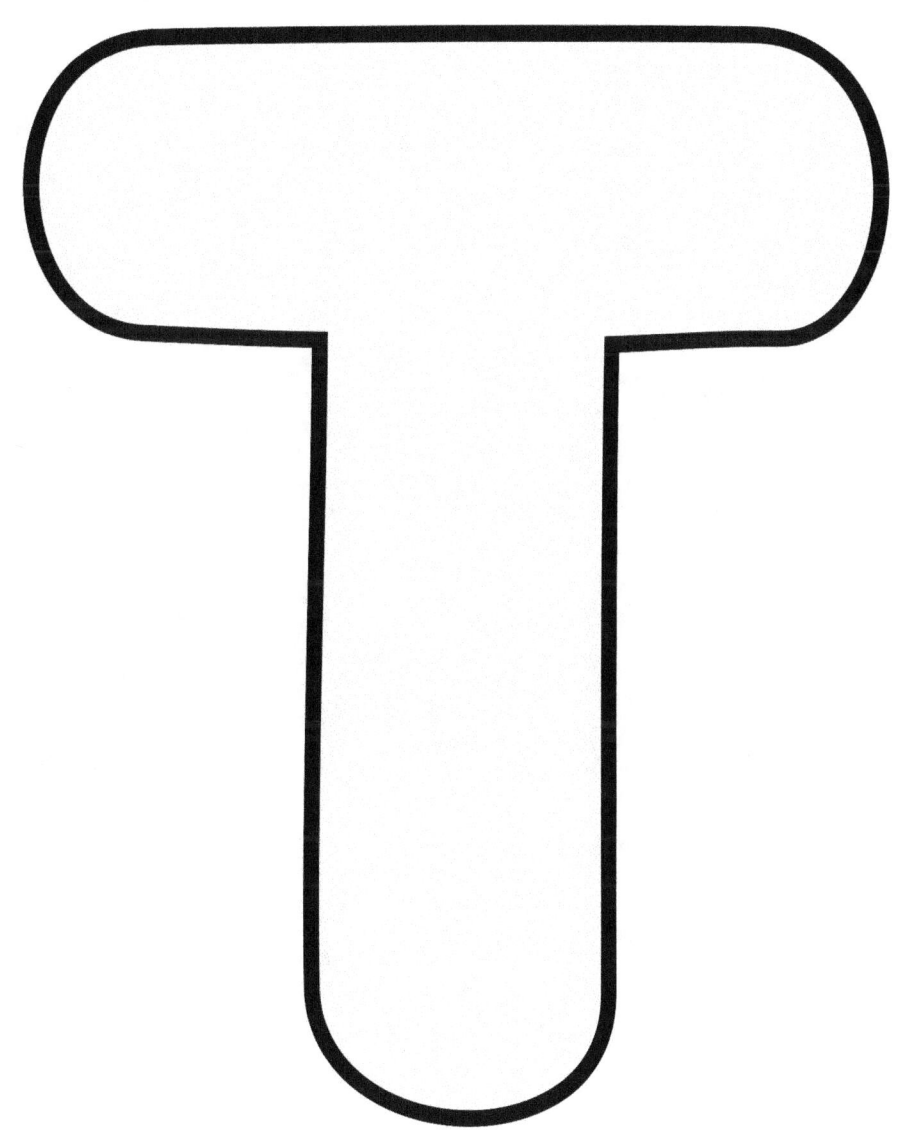

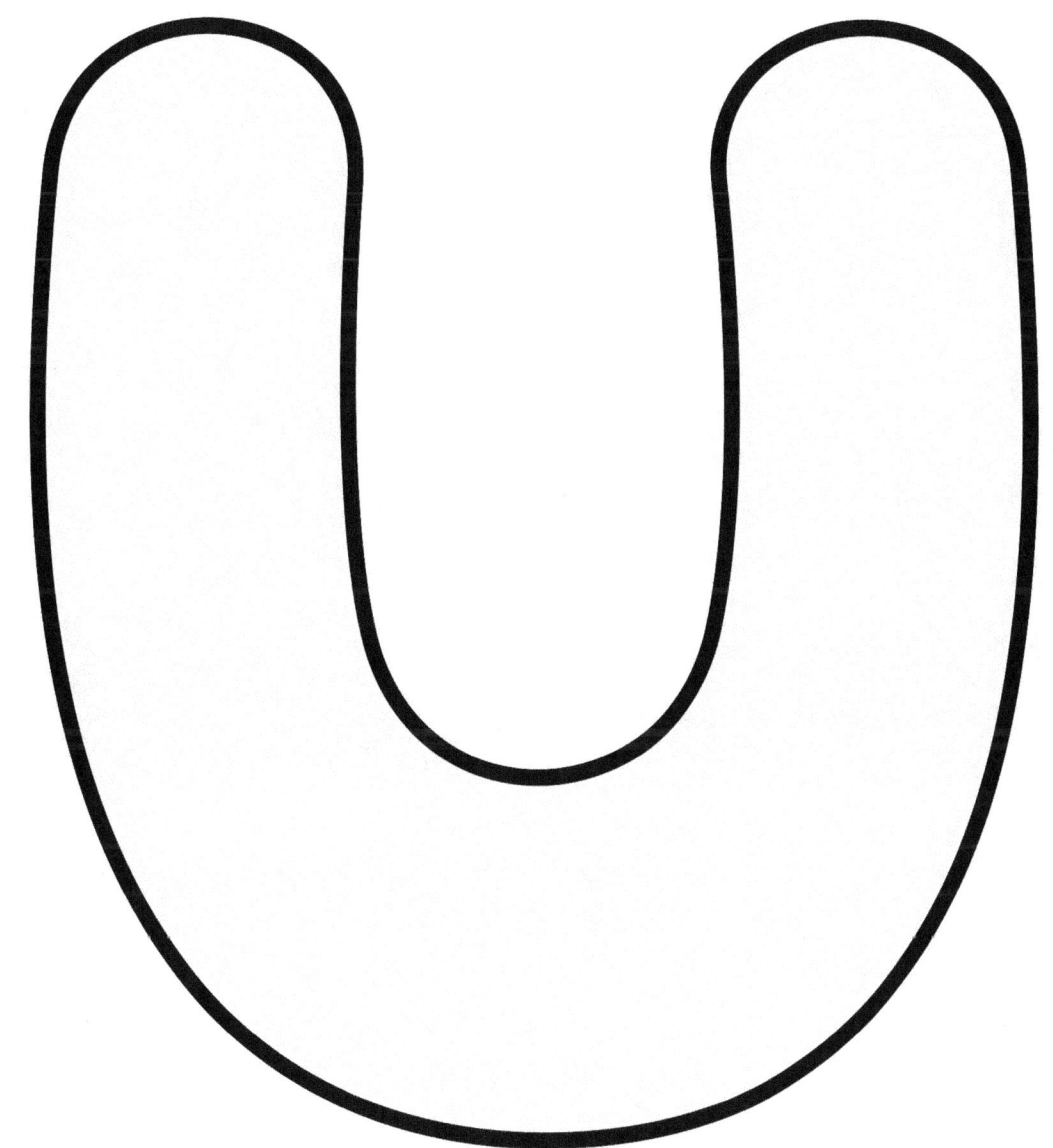

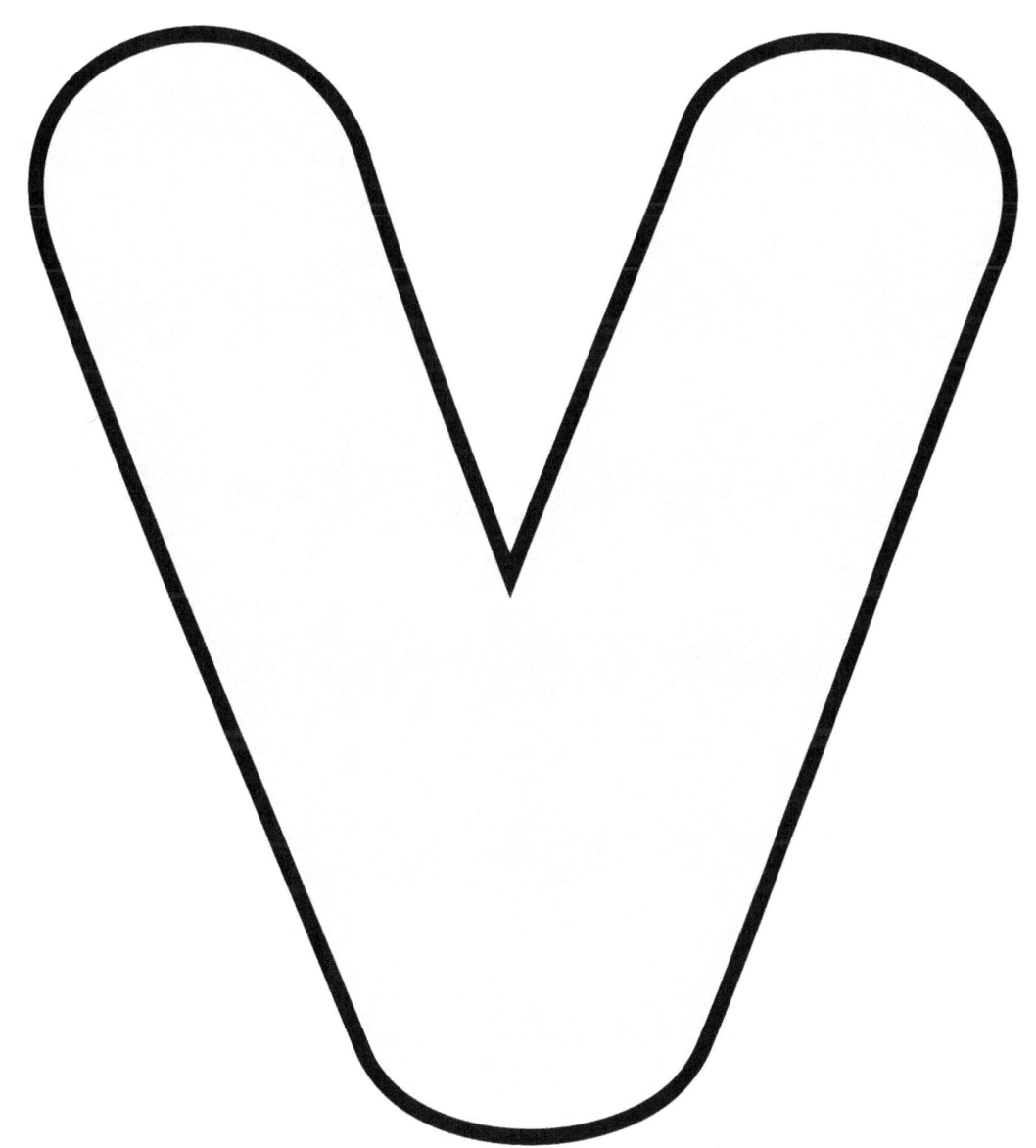

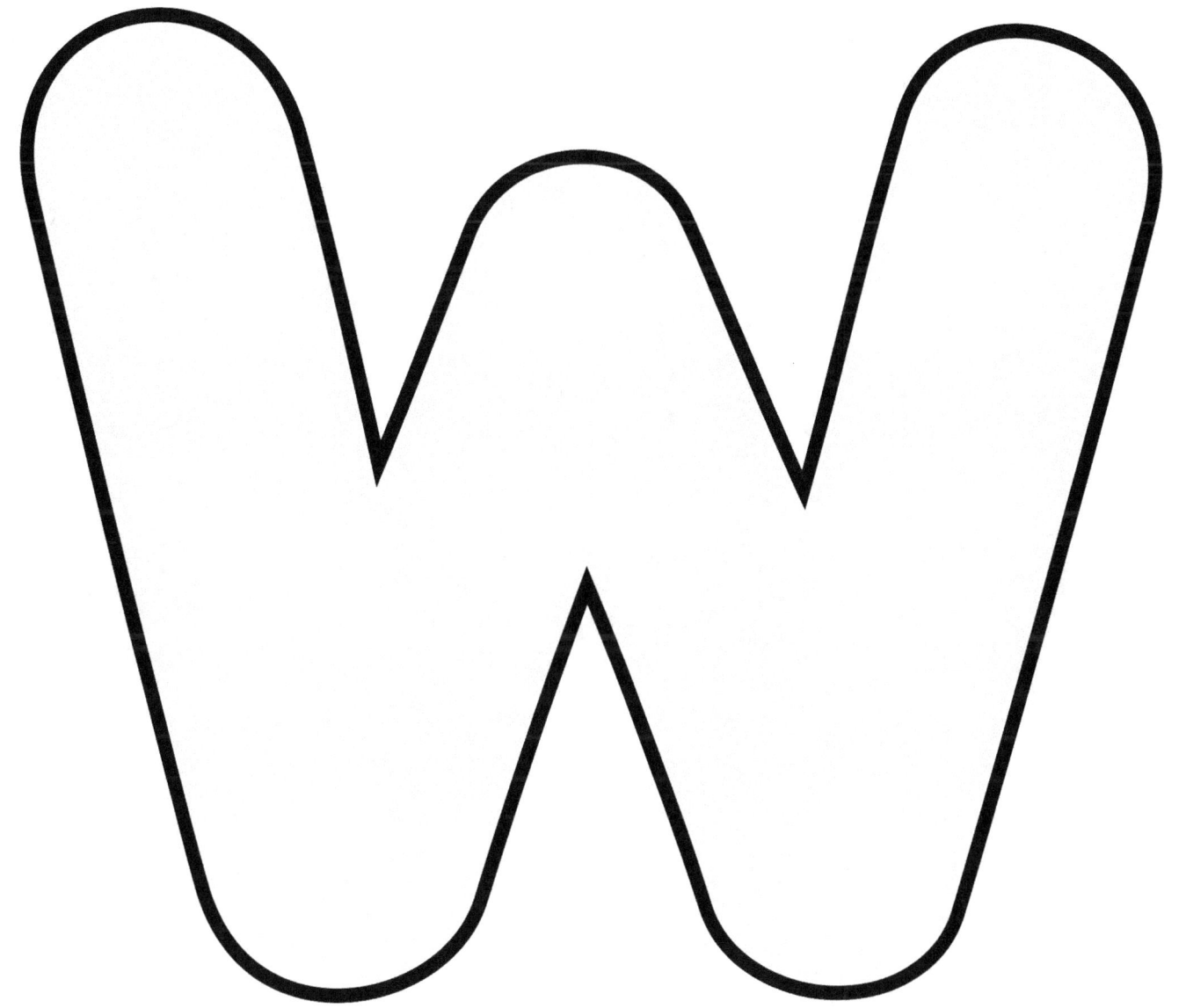

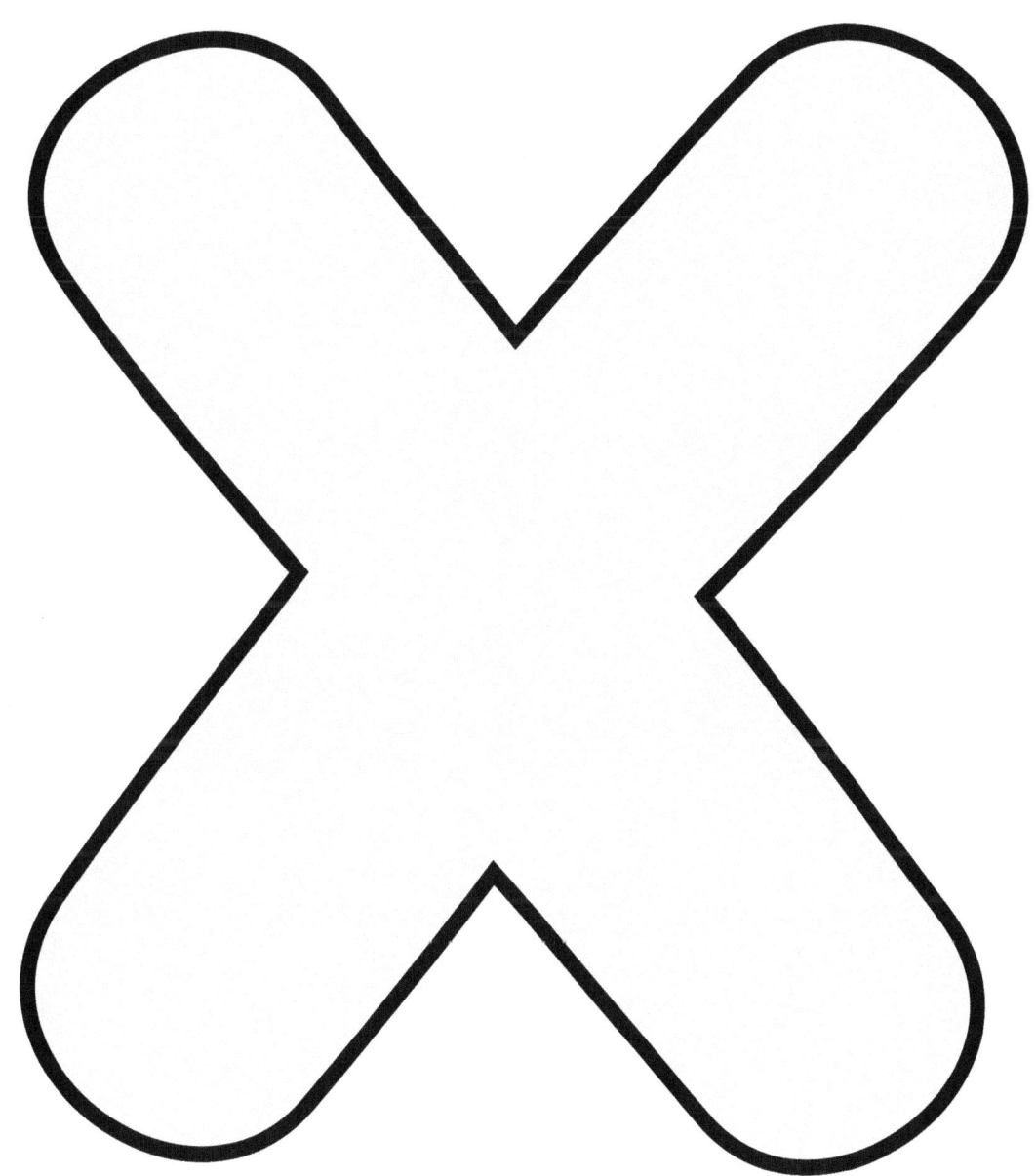

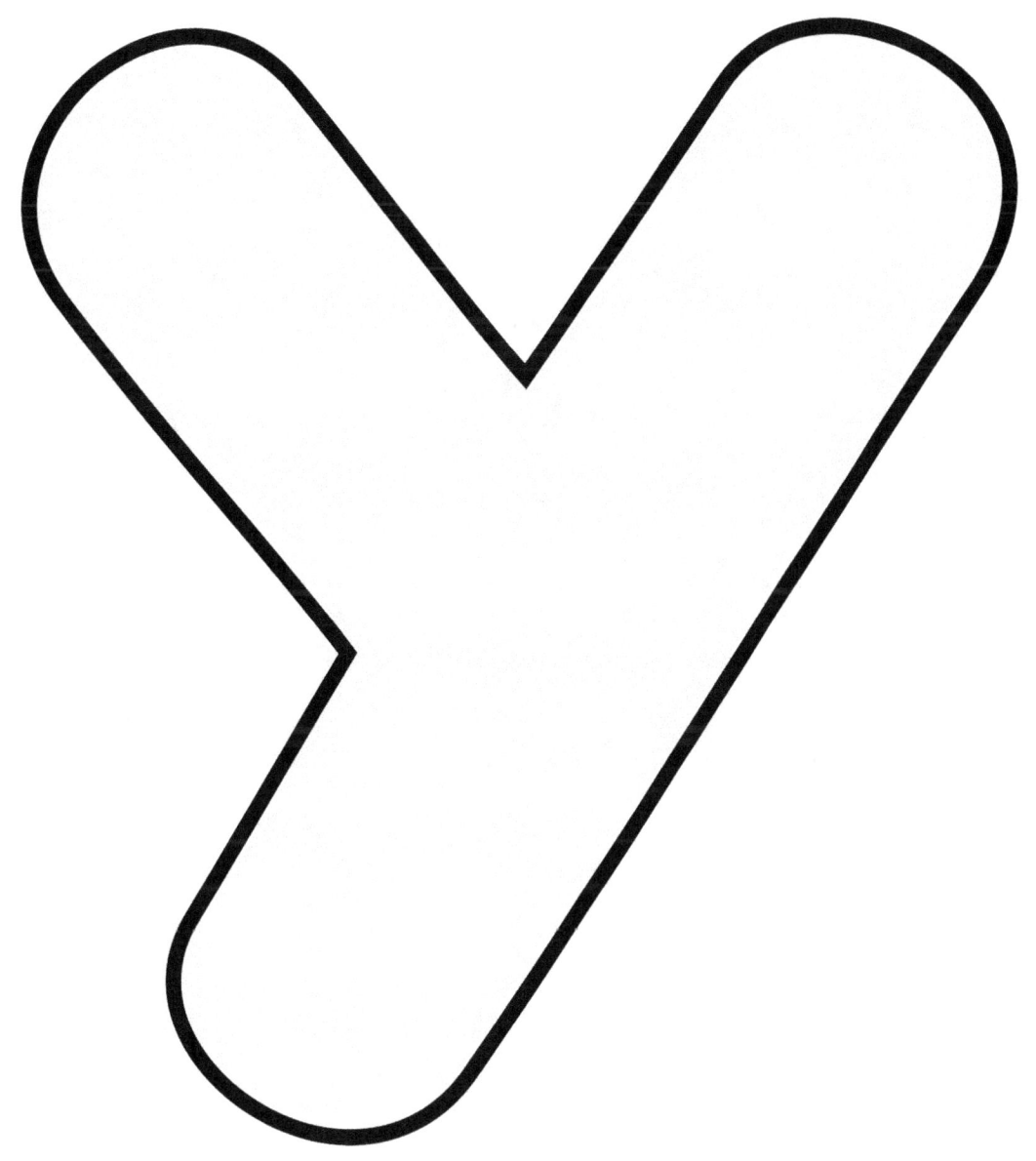

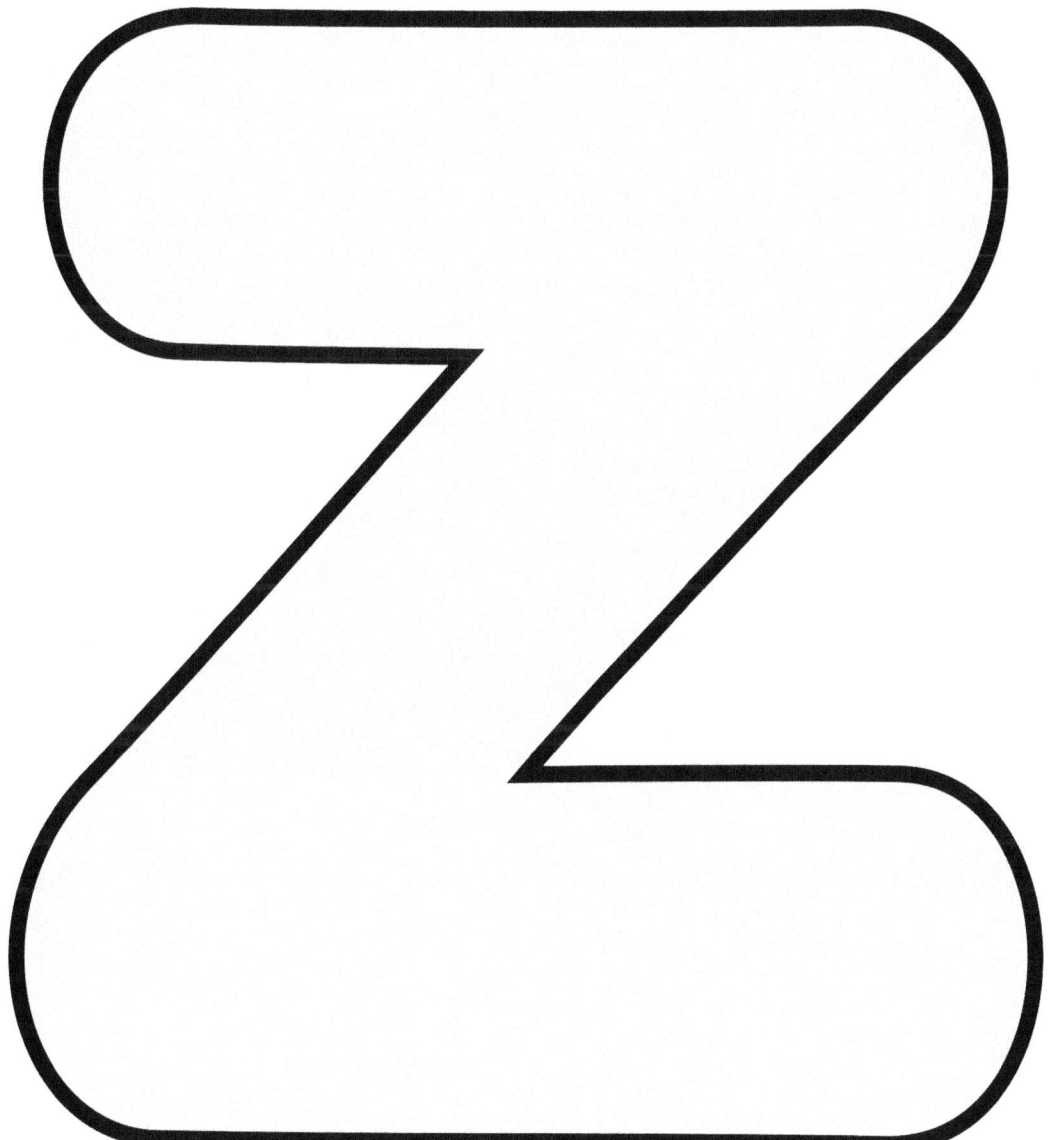

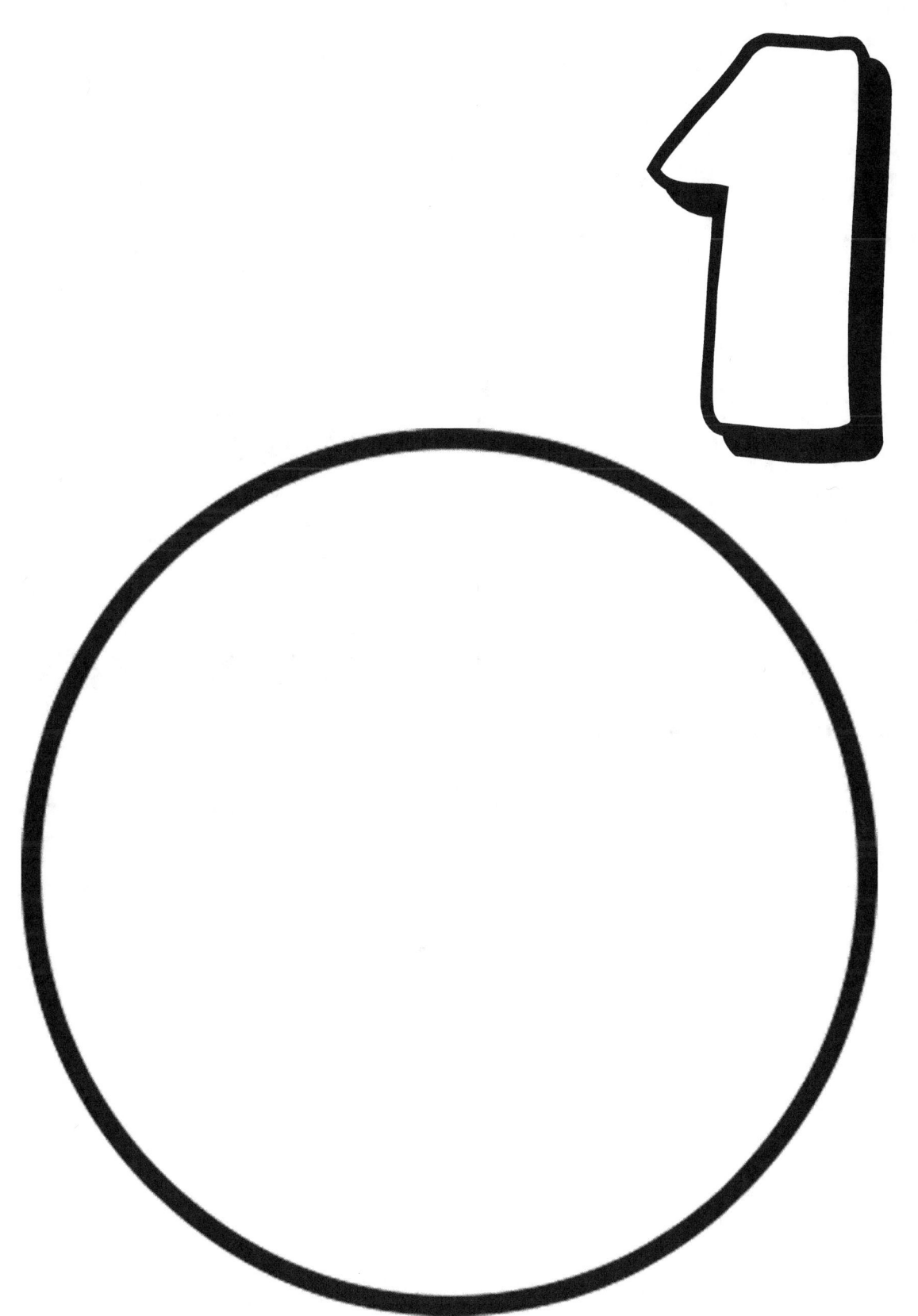

2

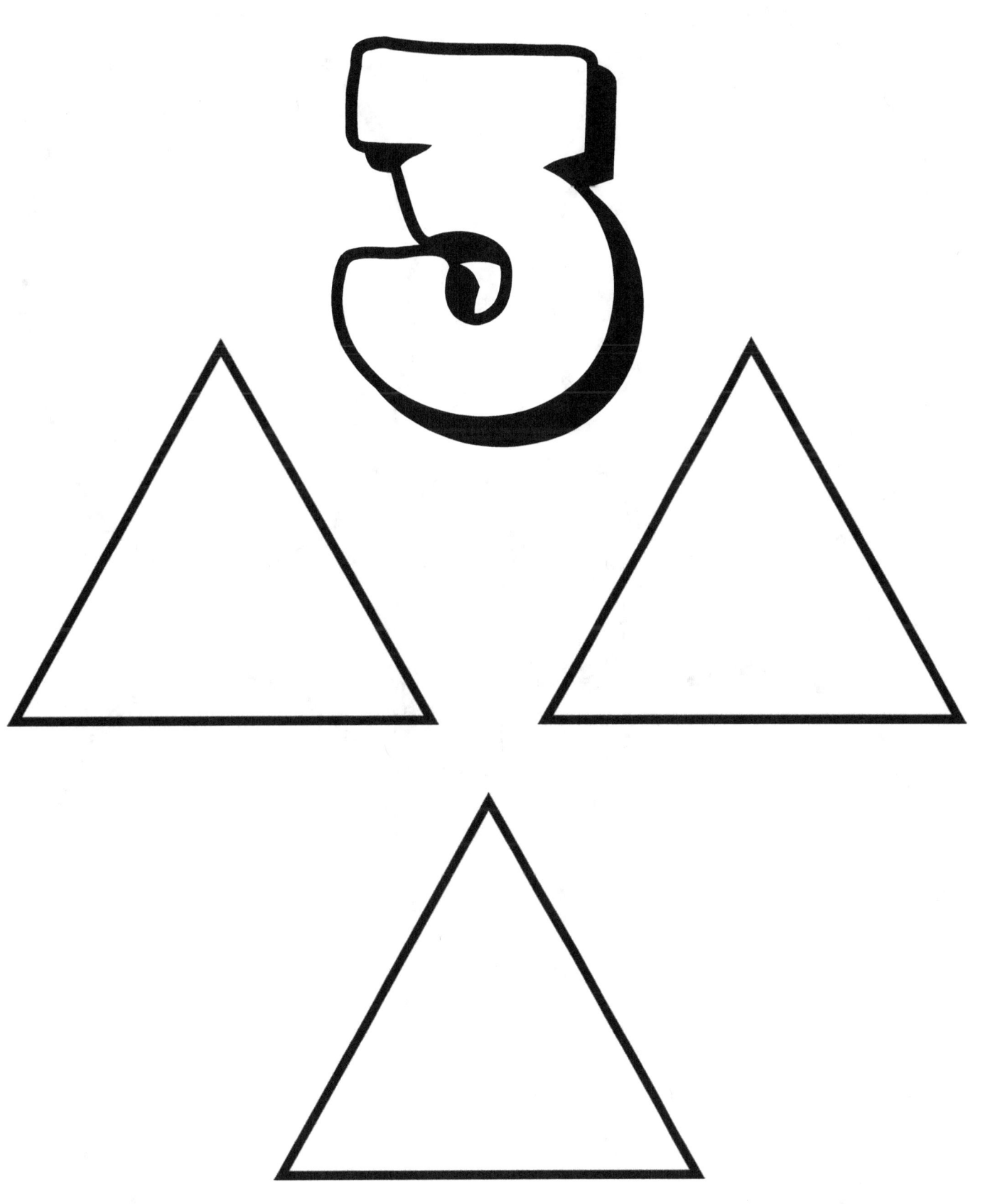

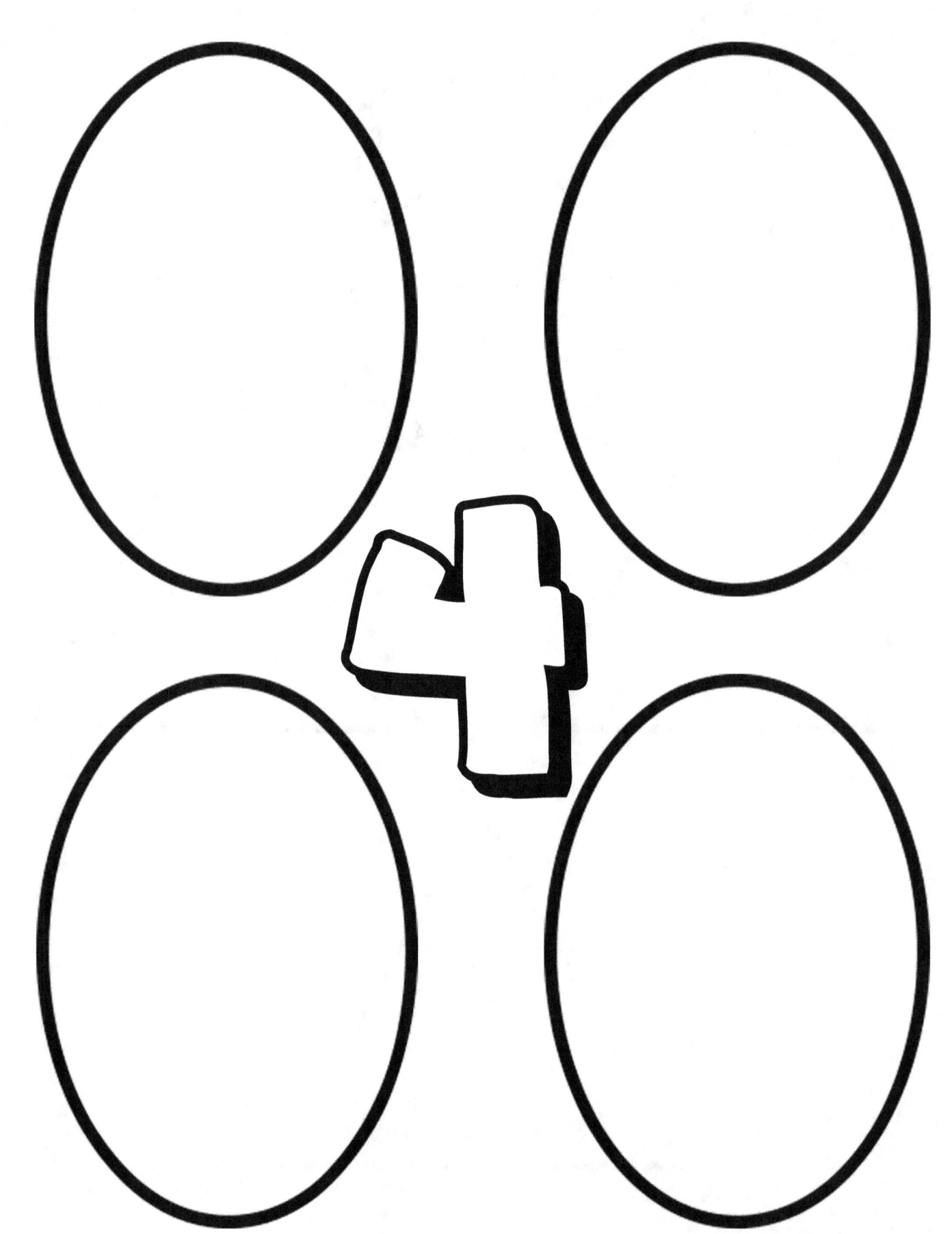

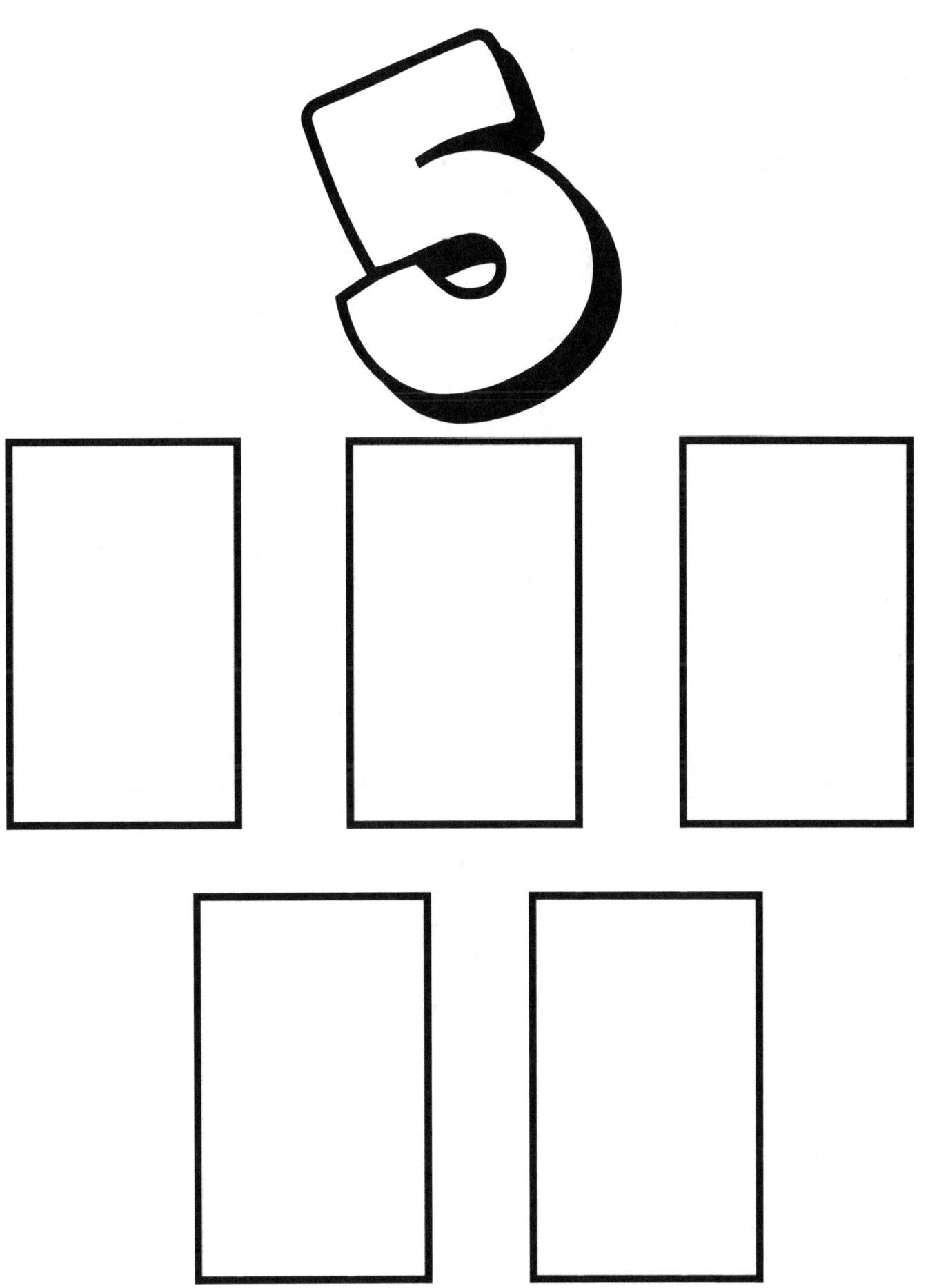

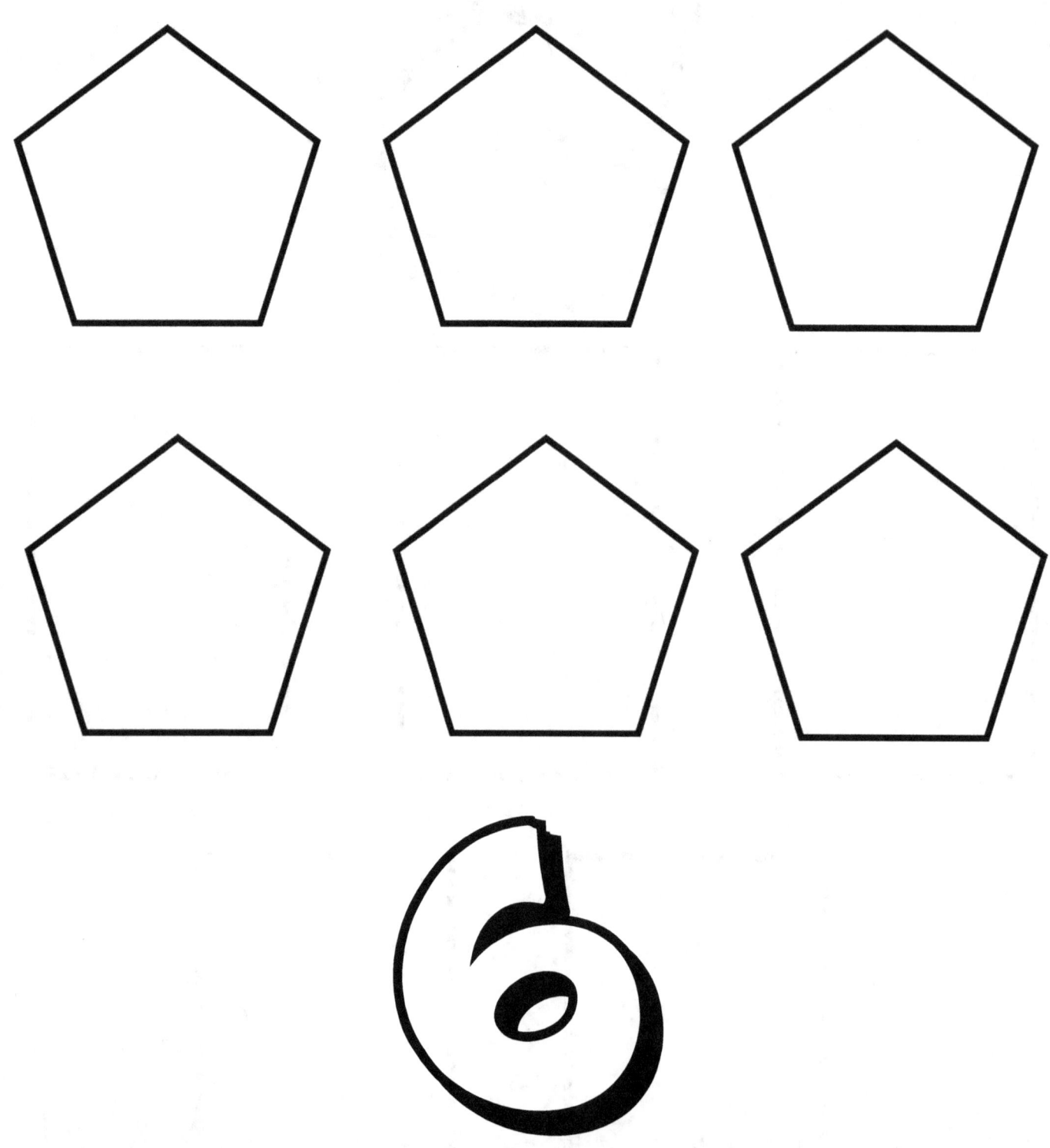

www.ingramcontent.com/pod-product-compliance
Lightning Source LLC
Chambersburg PA
CBHW062114220526
45471CB00010B/3730